Introduction

Alan Cooper

Back in 1965 the Rolling Stones' '(I can't get no) Satisfaction' stridently proclaimed that both radio and TV advertising left a lot to be desired. The information imparted on radio was useless and failed to *fire the imagination:* the presenter on TV selling soap powder guaranteed to make your shirts really white was the wrong role model, *he can't be a man.* Advertising was failing to understand, and tap into, its target audience and the result – *no satisfaction* – dissatisfied consumers.

Unbeknown to Mick and Keith, a quiet revolution in the way advertising was developed in agencies sparked into life a few years later. Account planning strove to make advertising better and more effective by introducing consumers and their attitudes into the advertising development process – no more *useless information. How to Plan Advertising* is a review of the principles and practice of account planning in the late 1990s.

The book is written for anyone who is interested in the way in which advertising is developed in agencies. Nowadays planners are, or at least a planning approach is, heavily involved in most advertising. Thus, the appeal of this book should extend across all those who work in, or with, advertising agencies in the UK, and indeed, the entire world. Beyond that, this book is an important reference for all students of business and marketing who want to know more about advertising.

How the book was written

How to Plan Advertising is very much a practical, how-to-do-it guide to planning and evaluating advertising. It has been written by the leading practitioners in their fields – the 'household names' of the advertising world. Their experience in advertising is immense. Cumulatively, the authors have spent over 250 years working in advertising and related fields. If this time was stretched back from the publication date of the book this would equate to a few decades before America ceased being a British colony! The book is written from practical and personal perspectives. The content is not only comprehensive but also thought-provoking. The authors have not reached their current exalted positions by simply adhering to accepted systems: they have challenged, innovated and improved, and this is represented in their chapters.

At another level, however, the book describes the thinking and processes that happen continuously in the country's best advertising agencies. It is a clear, practical reference crammed full with tips and guidelines that can be applied by planners everywhere.

The first *How to Plan Advertising* was published in 1987. The ensuing ten years have seen immense change in advertising and planning. This is demonstrated in the scope and content of this book which is very much enlarged from the earlier volume. New thinking and practice is written about in the core stages of the planning process. Completely new chapters have been introduced to reflect how the planning approach is extending across other areas of business.

How has account planning developed?

Advertising is a big business. Advertising is an exceedingly big business. Currently, worldwide expenditure on advertising is approximately $250 billion. This is equivalent to half of China's GDP (Gross Domestic Product).

Advertising is highly significant globally in, at least, three different ways. Its *business significance* stems from its ability to drive a brand's sales and generate incremental profit. It has a *corporate significance* in that advertising can be a highly visible public statement of a company's beliefs and attitudes that often spans the entire globe (e.g. Coca Cola, McDonald's, British Airways). Advertising has a *cultural significance* as it can promote, or lead, popular culture (e.g. Levi's, Nike).

Increasingly, at the centre of advertising stands the approach of planning. However, account planning as a discipline, and planner as a job title, is relatively new in advertising terms: it has not yet celebrated its 30th birthday. There are still probably no more than 2,000 people in the entire world who would specifically call themselves an account planner.

So what does this small but, apparently, highly significant group of people do?

First, it has to be said that account planners did not invent the planning approach in advertising. Creative geniuses had been planning intuitively for a long time. If planners are said to have started out by uncovering and involving the consumer perspective in advertising development, then one of the godfathers of our business had, in reality, been already doing this for a long time.

'At the heart of an effective creative philosophy is the belief that nothing is so powerful as an insight into human nature, what compulsions drive a man, what instincts dominate his action, even though his language so often camouflages what really motivates him.'

Bill Bernbach

The role of account planners has moved on since the initial description of 'representing the voice of the consumer' was coined in the 1970s. Nowadays, I can't imagine that much advertising is developed without a consumer perspective being represented, even if account planning has not been used specifically.

By the mid-1980s account planning had evolved. It could then have been defined as 'fostering an attitude in the agency of what is important to bring about effective advertising'. At the core of this remained the task of understanding the consumer to unearth a key insight for advertising. In addition, it recognised the importance of advertising cutting through and connecting with its audience, and the need to demonstrate advertising's effectiveness in the marketplace.

What is account planning now?

As the millennium approaches the increasing rapidity of change in business and marketing is one of the catalysts of change for advertising agencies and planners. The speed with which competitors can copy products and bring them to market, coupled with the down-sizing of many marketing departments, is laying ever more importance on strategic thinking in helping to differentiate brands.

The mushrooming of media channels can be viewed as both an enemy and an ally in effectively connecting with a target audience. Choice of media will increasingly come before, and help shape, creative strategy rather than vice versa. The vital role of clever *media thinking* is rising up companies' agendas. In parallel with this, communication ideas (i.e. creativity that works in any medium) are becoming more of a prerequisite than simply advertising ideas.

In this country there is a whole generation of adults who have grown up with intrusive television advertising surrounding them. Their children have grown up in a society in which advertising is very much part of popular culture: it is talked about on TV, in newspapers, at work, in pubs and in the playground. Consumers know the game of advertising well – and often better than some advertisers! In this climate *thinking about advertising* in its own right – as an end in itself, not simply as a means to an end – is vital. Exploring different ways in which advertising can work is critical in keeping ahead of the competition and exceeding (rather than just matching) consumer expectations.

Innovative *strategic thinking, media thinking* and *advertising thinking* are aspects in which planners are, or should be, becoming involved. These are the routes to achieving competitive advantage for advertisers today – just as unearthing a fresh consumer insight or perspective was in the early days of planning.

So a definition of planning for the new millennium could be helping make advertising (or communication) better by providing an holistic understanding of consumers and brands and the ways that they can connect. 'Holistic' refers to understanding the consumer as a complete person, not simply as a user of a particular product or brand.

A framework of the target audience's lifestyle, attitudes, fears, hang-ups etc. is important for the creatives to tap into and, so, bring the brand closer to the consumer than any of its competitors. The connection is both content (i.e. brand benefits and values) and channel (i.e. media).

A thorough reading of this book is an important aid to understanding how to succeed in this brave new world.

The structure of the book

For most who are reading this book the basic stages of planning in an advertising agency will be self-evident. This book follows the basic sequence of tasks that a planner is concerned with in the process of developing and evaluating advertising.

The opening chapter sets the scene by describing the role and importance of planning in advertising agencies. It sets out where planning has come from, where it might go to and the challenges it faces along the way. For those readers who are about to embark on a career in advertising this chapter will help you decide if planning is right for you.

The next two chapters are accounts of the 'front end' of the advertising process. They help identify and define a role for advertising – what it can do well for a brand – and crystallise the best approaches to developing the core strategy. The strategy is the basic building block of any brand's advertising.

Chapters 4 and 5 cover the process of turning the advertising strategy into the most inspiring brief for the creative department to work from. (Although this book is written about planners and planning it should never be forgotten that the creative end product is the most important aspect of any agency.) Both perspectives on creative briefs and briefing are represented. 'What should planners do' is written by a planner and 'What do creatives want' is described from a creative's perspective.

The subsequent chapter deals with the often sensitive area of how planners can help to nourish and protect the creative idea prior to it appearing in the media. Many people, both inside the agency and the client company, use research to gain reassurance about the potential of the creative route – this chapter describes how this process should be best approached.

Chapter 7 documents the various ways planners can evaluate how the advertising is working. This generates both objective proof of effectiveness to the client and provides guidance for the first stage of the next planning cycle.

The last four chapters are testimony to how far planning has developed in the last ten years. The topics were barely mentioned at all in the original publication and now they have become so important that they deserve whole chapters devoted to them. Media is not only an important area for planners to understand but it is vital to incorporate it in strategy development and creative briefing. This chapter equips the planner with practical knowledge and provokes him, or her, to consider media – rather than leave it entirely to media departments or media agencies. Many of the practices used in planning purely domestic advertising have to be re-worked and adapted for multi-national advertising. Nevertheless, international planners must always set their sights on the highest common factor, rather than lowest common denominator. How to go about achieving this is outlined in Chapter 9.

Chapters 10 and 11 demonstrate that planners' work extends beyond the boundaries of the advertising agency. Many clients regard planners as adjuncts to their marketing department (or substitutes for them if they don't have one). Furthermore, agencies constantly strive to prove their worth to their clients beyond advertising – and how they can take their creative idea outside above-the-line media. The penultimate chapter provides practical guidance in these areas. The book's finale takes a look at planning outside advertising agencies and documents how the approach is used in other communication industries.

Finally, as you read this book you will recognise that the authors have written from their own perspectives and in their own words. Although, as editor, I have attempted to minimise overlap and duplication of content I have not set myself the brief of achieving a uniform writing style. Indeed, I think that this heterogeneity of literary style adds to the book's appeal and reflects the different traits of planners.

1 The planning context

High noon for the high ground

M. T. Rainey

Introduction

Like the video, the microwave, the cashpoint and increasingly the mobile phone in our everyday lives, it is hard for most of us today to imagine what agency life was like before planning. Yet the discipline of planning in agencies was equally an *invention:* a piece of advertising technology. Unlike many other modern inventions, however, planning was not a labour-saving device. It was not designed to make agency life easier and more convenient. In fact, if anything, planning added cost to the agency's overheads, time to the advertising development process and often controversy and debate to its resolution.

Yet against these odds, from its beginnings 30 years ago at BMP and JWT, planning has moved from being futuristic (in the 1970s); fashionable (in the 1980s); to being a fully functional fact of agency life in the 1990s – albeit in different forms and within different structures.

Planning can and should take no small credit for helping to sustain the high quality of British advertising over that period by building an effectiveness culture in British agencies which is not at odds with – and which in fact is dependent on – innovation and creativity in advertising.

Planning is a uniquely British invention, yet it is now present in various shapes and forms in agencies in the US, France, Germany, Italy, Scandinavia, The Netherlands, Australia, India, Hong Kong, South Africa and probably many other countries. It is estimated that almost 200 UK trained planners currently work abroad.

Planning has come a long way and has had a wide influence. It has made a difference; to advertising and its role in our culture; to agencies; to brands and to businesses. People who are part of it can be proud, and young people contemplating a career in planning today should feel excited.

In my recent experience, however, I have sensed a kind of complacency or certainly lack of passion about planning, particularly among new and younger planners. Certainly I have noticed that many of them do not know the history or the circumstances of planning's development; and many are not familiar with the names of its pioneers and have not read the texts and papers which defined and informed its growth. I sense a loss of evangelism, a diminishing of purpose and a fragmentation of method. *The risk in taking planning's history for granted is that we marginalise its future.*

Because it is also true that the advertising industry is now changing faster and more significantly than at any time in its past. *Planning must change or be changed.* It would be ironic if 'planners' were the last to know.

An approach

So, in writing this chapter on 'the planning context' I have chosen not to attempt to replicate or better the excellent pamphlet published by the APG called 'What is Account Planning?'.

Certainly a brief review of the chapter headings of this book will outline *what* planning actually does in an agency, and my colleagues will provide state of the art insight and best practice instruction on the *'how to'* of planning.

I will therefore try to give a perspective on the following two issues:

Why do we have Account Planning?
- by revisiting the origins of planning and pointing to the contributions that excited and incited the planners of my generation – in the hope that in some small way the pioneering spirit can be rekindled.

Where is Account Planning going?
- by raising the issues which face planning today in our fast-changing industry – in the belief that they represent new and significant challenges for the pioneers of tomorrow.

PART I: THE QUESTION 'WHY?'

Was there life before planning?

Yes, but not as we know it.

To understand why planning has prevailed and thrived, and to know how we must evolve it, we should surely remind ourselves of why it was invented in the first place.

In the 1960s, insightful advertising thinkers and practitioners, most famously Bill Bernbach at Doyle Dane Bernbach in the US, began to reject vociferously the frightening and archaic concept of the passive consumer and the notion that advertising *does things to* people. They replaced it with the concept of an active, complex and essentially disinterested consumer *doing things with* advertising. 'Distinctiveness' was added to 'relevance' as a dimension of how advertising works and as a necessary condition for advertising effectiveness. This created a recognition of the two-way relationship between consumer and advertiser and simultaneously, a *requirement for creativity in advertising.*

Yet in America today, in spite of the best efforts of Bill Bernbach and more recently Jay Chiat, there is still the well-entrenched belief that there are two kinds of advertising: creative advertising and advertising that sells. In Britain, however, we believe in the creative imperative, not the creative option, as a requirement for effectiveness.

The difference between the development of our two advertising cultures from the same point of insight, is the difference that planning has made.

This difference is also clear in the role of advertising within our national cultures. In the UK, people generally enjoy and approve of advertising, while in the US it is generally considered intrusive and insulting to the intelligence.

Life without planning

In the US the model of the passive consumer had led to, and arguably was led by, a mechanistic research culture, in which over-simplistic stimulus-response 'testing' promised to be able to measure *whether ads worked* in a laboratory situation. This was irresistibly appealing to clients and fostered a culture of 'hard sell' advertising in which the client's 'unique selling proposition' was straightforwardly presented and assumed to be noticed, believed and acted upon if it was clearly and repeatedly communicated.

Advertising development and evaluation was effectively out of the hands of the agencies and controlled by hugely powerful research companies like ARS and Burke, each with spurious one-dimensional models of how advertising worked, and with years of comparative back data to provide a semblance of validity. Tracking was almost unheard of. Qualitative research was anathema.

Luckily this kind of research culture had not yet gained a strong foothold in the UK, though things were heading that way. Agency research departments were still 'staff' functions, external to the process of advertising development, and providing data and research 'answers' in response to the questions and requests of account managers. There was also more and more data to be dealt with.

The planning breakthrough

Both Stephen King at JWT and Stanley Pollitt (then at Pritchard Wood) clearly recognised the flaws in this system: that the people who knew most about the issues – the researchers – were not party to the advertising decisions or the creative process; and the people most able to make the decisions – the account men – might be tempted by expediency, since, no matter how strong their strategic instincts, their first order of business was keeping the client happy. Clearly objectivity was not best served under those circumstances.

Both men had a vision to institutionalise 'objectivity' within the advertising *structure* by bringing research information more closely into the *process* of advertising. JWT coined the term 'account planning' and Stanley Pollitt took it to its natural and, at the time, radical conclusion with the launch of BMP and the introduction of the account planner.

The account planner at BMP worked shoulder to shoulder with account management and indeed with creative people as the consumers' representative on the team. Planning was a fully integrated line management function with its own proactive roles and responsibilities and a direct relationship with the client.

Coining the term 'relevant distinctiveness' as its philosophy of effective advertising, BMP required its planners to bring consumer research to bear at *all* stages of the advertising process, impinging on both content issues (relevance or 'strategy'), form issues (distinctiveness or 'execution') and of course on evaluation. As a member of the team rather than an outside 'supplier', this brought the planner to the very heart of the advertising development process and into a very influential position in the agency.

The planner was to be an expert in the consumer's relationship with brands and advertising both generally and specifically to the accounts he or she was working on. Although the job was to *use* research, not to *do* research, BMP believed that planners

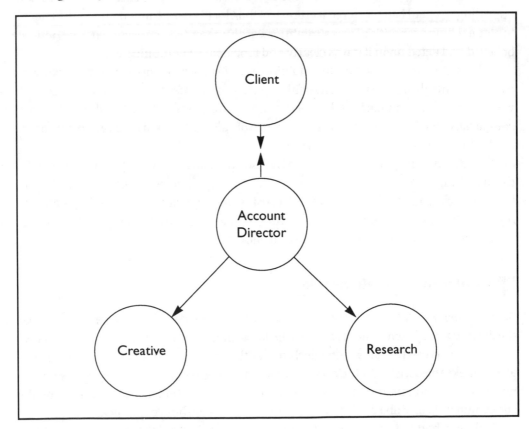

Figure 1.1: Agency structure before planning

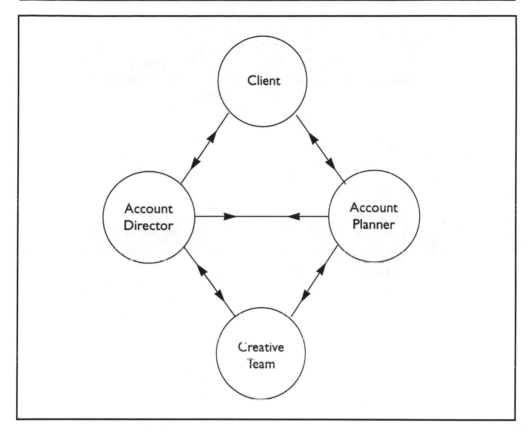

Figure 1.2: Agency structure after planning

should conduct their own 'groups' as only they would have the right interpretative skills for advertising decisions.

Obviously this hybrid person required both advertising sensitivities and research skills – not a combination that existed in many people in the industry at the time. So BMP spotted, hired and trained them.

In the early 1980s, a planning training document at Benton & Bowles was prefaced with the following caution:

'Planning is a development in advertising and NOT a development in research. Failure to remember that may seriously damage your health.'

Obvious as this distinction may appear today, it was fundamental to the new culture of planning and to recruiting a new breed of person with the right skills and sensibilities for the job.

As BMP became a very successful agency and JWT continued to go from strength to strength, other agencies soon followed suit. Exciting new creative shops were formed

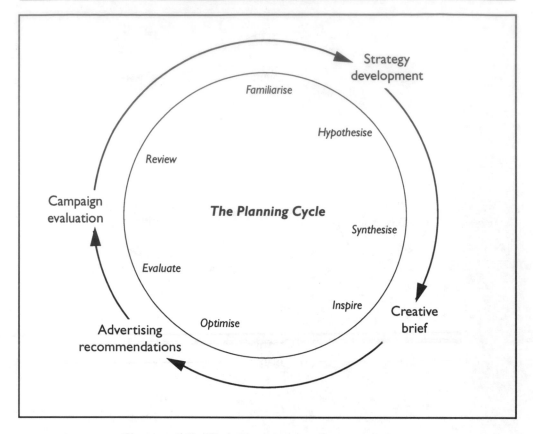

Figure 1.3: The advertising development process

with planners in their management structure (most notably BBH) and eventually even the large multinationals found a role, even a competitive need, for planning in their full service offerings.

It's difficult to imagine now just how innovative and brave this 'invention' of planning was at the time and how it shook the foundations of agency life and agency politics. In particular, the involvement of planners in using research to help develop creative work was radical at the time and is still the point of departure for some agencies today.

In the previous edition of this book Don Cowley made the following point:

'The profound difference that account planning brought to the process was a method that was consumer led. Since advertisements are supposedly designed wholly and inescapably to influence the consumption behaviour of members of the public, you might be forgiven for thinking that this is not much of a breakthrough. But surprisingly enough it was, and still is for many parts of the advertising world, a revolutionary and controversial philosophy.'

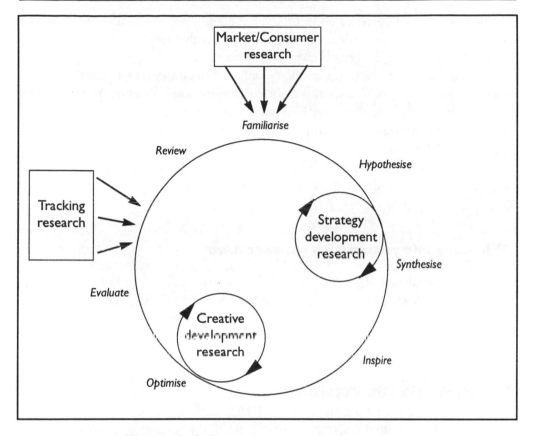

Figure 1.4: Research input to the planning cycle

Perhaps more than anything else, however, planning really required a commitment by agency leaders to an effectiveness culture. Stanley Pollitt (1979) wrote:

> 'Planning can only work when there is a total agency management commitment to getting the advertising right at all costs. Getting it right being more important than maximising agency profits, keeping clients happy or creating an agency shop window for distinctive looking advertising.'

It took precisely this kind of management commitment to the integration and institutionalisation of 'objectivity' into the agency, in the form of a new breed of agency person and a new kind of advertising process, to stave off the worst excesses of mechanistic research and to replace them with a stronger, better, more enlightened, more effective culture.

This was something the Americans neither acknowledged nor attempted at the time. With Bernbach's words ringing in their ears American advertising culture and quality floundered in the 1970s and 1980s until the import of planning by Chiat/Day in the early 1980s finally spawned a planning culture in the 1990s. This has helped regional creative hot shops to become powerful domestic and even international advertising players. It is also not a coincidence that the US is currently enjoying something of a creative renaissance in international awards shows.

This kind of culture, however, is still optional and not imperative in the US. It is still not mainstream. The reason for this is the continuing power of a combative research industry supported by multinational companies and condoned by multinational agencies; using mechanistic and counter-intuitive methods of predicting or measuring advertising's effectiveness.

Planning could never have thrived to the extent that it has in the UK, without the co-operation and academic contribution of our own research industry, to which we owe a huge debt of gratitude.

Planning and research – a collaboration

The preoccupation of the UK advertising and research industry at the time of planning's inception and growth, was in trying to better understand and demonstrate *how* advertising worked. This contrasted sharply with the US focus on *whether* ads worked. Another major difference was that the advertising and research industries in the UK *collaborated* on the problem.

A new manifesto for advertising research

In 1974 the IPA published a seminal text by Alan Hedges called 'Testing to Destruction'. This was a powerful and convincing indictment of the mechanistic testing culture. Hedges wrote:

> 'It is not possible to make a realistic test of the effectiveness of advertising in a laboratory situation in advance of real life exposure. Until this simple but uncomfortable truth is grasped much advertising research will go on being sterile and unproductive.'

The book was also an impressive dissertation on the consumers' relationship with products, brands and advertising and the proper and appropriate uses of research in advertising.

> 'The most important contribution research can make to increasing the selling effectiveness of advertising is at the planning stage . . . research can heighten our understanding of the market and of the consumer so that we can better understand the job that advertising has to do and the climate in which it has to operate. If this is done properly it not only guides and stimulates the creative process but also provides a much better basis for eventual decisions about the likely worth of a campaign.'

This was effectively a blueprint for planning and the research methods that would best serve it.

A new methodology for advertising research

In the 1960s, the Schlackman organisation was pioneering the use of qualitative research in understanding consumer psychology and decision-making. This kind of research methodology had previously only been used within academic environments in clinical and social psychology. There was an increasing appreciation that qualitative research, specifically focus group discussions, was reliable and valid and provided invaluable diagnostic data simply not available by other means.

Pioneers like Stephen Wells, Judie Lannon, Roy Langmaid, Wendy Gordon and many others, developed qualitative techniques specifically to aid advertising decisions and contributed much understanding and insight about how advertising worked in the form of published papers and training events. Importantly, they were instrumental in educating and inspiring a new generation of planners in qualitative research.

Quantitative support for the creative imperative

There were also many key lessons being learned about how advertising worked through a growing body of knowledge from advertising tracking. Quantitative tracking studies were starting to illustrate the relationships between different kinds of advertising messages, different kinds of advertising forms, different media weights and different media patterns on key 'intervening variables' like advertising and brand, awareness and attitudes.

Gordon Brown of Millward Brown published a number of important and influential papers on this learning in the late 1970s and early 1980s. These studies generally supported the creative imperative. Data began to indicate that up to 40 per cent of the variability in advertising performance on tracking studies was due to the creativity or 'cut through' of the advertising. Tracking data also started to build an appreciation that what was interesting or 'creative' in the advertising needed to be linked to the brand itself in order for information and attributes to be successfully transferred. This led planners and creative people away from gratuitous, 'tacked-on' or irrelevant creativity – towards the search for the branded or ownable idea.

Recognition of advertising literacy

Out of many papers published in the 1980s, two deserve a mention. One was given by Dr Terry O'Brien at an APG event in 1980, and was called 'What Consumers Bring To Advertising'. In it he attempted to describe and delineate what he called the *transcendent factors* in advertising. This was basically the beginning of our recognition of the sophisticated *consumer of advertising.*

In the context of creative development research, planners and qualitative researchers were starting to notice that consumers were increasingly 'judging' a specific advertisement or advertising approach not only in terms of its functional information and emotional appeal but also in the context of all other advertising.

Consumers were aware of, and in collusion with, advertising's intent; they were learning about advertising and the conventions it used and were able to make rules and generalisations about it which 'transcended' the advertiser's intentions. Issues like advertising context, fashions and styles in advertising, what the advertising doesn't say; production values or 'quality', recognition of intent, effort after meaning etc. are all discussed in O'Brien's paper.

This was the stuff that good advertising people tended to know instinctively, but which was very hard even for planners to explain and justify to clients in creative presentations because it was so 'amorphous' and apparently subjective.

To have these 'transcendent factors' documented by an objective and dispassionate outside researcher gave the concept of the 'advertising literate' consumer stature and credibility. It also helped give planners a missionary zeal to be instrumental in helping move advertising forward.

This concept of the 'advertising consumer' was expanded and elaborated on by Rod Meadows in his excellent paper published in *AdMap* in 1983 called 'They Consume Advertising Too'. In it he pleaded that advertising research, and the decisions made on the basis of it, should take into account the consumer's relationship with advertising and not just their relationship with the brand and category being represented.

> 'If research is to make a fully effective contribution to advertising development it has to be permitted to drill where the advertising literate consumer has moved to.'

All of these contributions, many from outside the advertising industry itself, helped support the concept of the creative imperative within an effectiveness culture. They gave planning a technical 'toolbox' and a unique skill set. They helped give planners the power of conviction and the rhetoric to persuade clients to buy better, more creative, more effective advertising.

Planning divergence

It was around the late 1980s, however, that planning practice and certainly planning styles started to diverge.

'The Ad Tweaker'

There were those planners whose skill and interests lay in helping their agencies develop and sell increasingly entertaining, unexpected and colloquial advertising that recognised and indeed played to the sophistication of the consumer – effectively entering into a contract of *complicity* with them. Typically this kind of planner 'hung out' in and with the creative department and has rather pejoratively been termed the 'ad tweaker'.

Always in demand, the 'ad tweaker' has seen a bit of a renaissance recently with the advent of the 'new lad' and the increasing tribalisation of youth culture. They (more likely he) may be typically found planning on booze, sports shoes, video games and soft drinks.

The speciality of the 'ad tweaker' is the supercynical, hyper-literate advertising consumer. And the logical conclusion of this collaboration between creatives and ad tweaking planners is the current fashion for 'lucid advertising': ads about advertising, ads about marketing, and ads about other ads.

While pejoratively described here, this is actually a valid function of planning if we continue to believe in the two-way nature of the advertiser/consumer relationship and the increasing advertising literacy of the consumer. Certainly some famous and highly effective advertising has come out it.

'The Storyteller'

In many agencies, however, this kind of extreme proximity to the creative process, and in fact to creative people, was too rich for the blood. Another type of planner evolved who tended to focus on enriching the front end of the process – by giving as full a picture as possible of the product and the consumer in the belief that the secret would lie in some quirky detail that would inspire the creative team.

This kind of planner might be termed 'the storyteller'. They would write the kind of briefs that told us what the target audience had for breakfast, even if they were advertising a bank. They were full of anecdotes about the consumer. They interrogated the product. They would unearth the fact that this running shoe had been worn by the only man to escape from Colditz or that this beer contained Serbo-Croatian hops.

And we can again see that some very interesting advertising has been informed by this kind of planning – especially in an environment in which products are becoming more and more commoditised, or in categories in which image and 'folklore' are just as valid discriminators as product characteristics, if not more so.

'The Grand Brand Strategist'

There was yet another type of planner whose remit tended to be defined and indeed confined by what might be called 'brand positioning'. This kind of planner would be extremely knowledgeable about the brand: its competitors; its market structure and dynamics; its products and of course its consumers. They would typically have a close relationship with the client who might consider him or her to be the fount of all wisdom.

Within the agency this kind of planner would tend to be a bit of an 'information guru' and out of all this information they would proscribe a clear direction or positioning for the brand, which was elaborately sold to the client. They would then typically pass the baton of the task on to the other members of the team.

Again, this is a valid, if narrow, application of planning and it no doubt suits some agency cultures.

Now almost certainly no single planner exclusively resides in any of these planning caricatures. More likely all of us have practised all of those kinds of planning at different times, on different accounts in different agencies and to suit the purposes of different clients. Yet tendencies towards these different planning styles are increasingly discernible in individual planners and between different agencies. They are probably not formalised but evolve to suit the agency culture and leadership, and to create or reinforce a point of difference.

While they all represent valid planning contributions they are really a retrenchment to 'corners' and may have begun to undermine or indeed evacuate the more important 'pivotal' role for planning in today's and tomorrow's communications industry.

PART 2: THE QUESTION 'WHERE?'

A weakening of purpose

Over the medium to long term, an emphasis on the 'ad tweaking' style of planning may have insidiously weakened the perceived objectivity of planning to clients and, therefore, reduced its power to sell and persuade. It also distances that planner from the strategic or front end of the process if the perception is that his answer is always to be found in 'form' not 'content'; in the 60-second commercial as opposed to the creative 'idea'.

Similarly, over time, an emphasis on the 'storytelling' style of planning may have created the perception that planners are about uncovering interesting information for advertising and not creating valuable insights for brands: more like a BBC researcher than an advertising expert.

Finally, a relegation of the planner to the high priest of positioning, leaves the field of advertising research open to outside third parties, and increasingly the very kind of third party that the invention of planning was designed to obstruct.

As a result of this evolution of planning into a divergence of method and style, two major challenges to traditional or 'ideal' planning are emerging.

The challenges to planning

1. *There is a gradual encroachment of US-style mechanistic advertising research methodologies into the UK marketing culture.*

Increasingly these are being used and often mandated on international business, by multinational companies and even by UK clients with no external pressure. Worse, they are being reinvented and endorsed by our own research industry, who should know better but who are finding it a very significant commercial opportunity.

Planners, and therefore agencies, are losing the high ground in advertising research. Advertising risks being 'tested to destruction'.

It is a challenge for today's planning pioneers to reignite the collaboration between the advertising and research industries; to find ways of addressing client needs for greater surety in an increasingly competitive and uncertain world, without prejudicing the creative imperative, which must surely now be greater than ever. There are a few sensitive quantitative pre-testing systems in existence, which have been designed by and are practised by ex-advertising planners.

It is also our responsibility in the advertising industry to continue to document our understanding of how advertising works, and indeed the many different ways that communication can work in the new media future.

2. Clients are beginning to look outside the agency for higher order thinking .

This is partly a result of planners and agencies being obsessed with execution and focusing on advertising strategies rather than brand ideas or communications ideas. This is happening at the same time as clients are moving more towards an integrated 'through the line' future.

It is undoubtedly also due, however, to the success of a number of high profile research and planning consultancies like Red Spider and Added Value, which started during the recession when fewer planners were being hired and trained by agencies. The recession has definitely led to a dearth of experienced senior planners in agencies and this vacuum is being filled by outside companies.

So, in this way planning is also in danger of losing the high ground in strategic thinking.

The challenge of the planning pioneers of tomorrow is to get it back. Not necessarily by displacing outside counsel, or certainly enlightened research input, but by a creating a new and unique role for planning which is much more relevant to today's market.

 ## new vision for planning

Perhaps research, which is about finding answers, really isn't the domain of the planner. It's not enough any more just to uncover a truth about a brand, or to ask consumers what they want, what they think or what they like. It's not enough even to understand *how* they think – because that insight is potentially also available to competitors.

Planning in today's communications industry surely isn't really about finding new answers – it isn't even really about discovery – it's about asking new questions.

People in advertising always speak rather witheringly about a scientific approach. *Yet the purest scientific method is highly creative. It is that of hypothesis testing.* The ability, on the basis of what we know, to imagine what we don't yet know: what doesn't yet exist or what could be. The creation of the 'What if' scenario. To step outside convention and constraint, not just in terms of advertising and communication structure and execution, but also in brand context, competitive alignment, category functionality and media deployment.

The invention and creation of new marketing scenarios, new brand visions and new communication paradigms can be the new remit for planning.

The need is there. Technology has facilitated a world of integrated brand communication. Media is fragmenting and multiplying like cell division. The internet and other interactive technologies change the contract between the brand and the consumer. *More than ever, clients need transformational ideas that transcend advertising.* Yet where does or can this kind of high concept creativity reside?

Certainly it should reside within what have traditionally been known as advertising agencies – because the UK agency tradition has always been driven by effectiveness and fuelled by creativity. Advertising agencies, unlike research and consulting companies, have always had to both solve the problem ***and*** create the solution. We have always had to take responsibility for the quality of both the input (strategy) ***and*** the output (execution). Our hearts and our minds therefore are uniquely in the right place.

Possibly, the opportunity lies with creative people. Certainly those who can step out of their reliance on craft creativity can step up to this new conceptual high ground. We already know that some of the best creative people have always been brilliant instinctive planners. However, a high level of market and brand literacy is required for this kind of creative remit not to result in gimmickry.

The most likely scenario though is that this opportunity for high concept creativity will create a new kind of planning and a new breed of planner, many of whom exist today.

At the risk of total vilification, *I believe that planning can be the new creativity or, at the very least, that planning can lead the new creativity.*

Agencies must offer, if not executional integration, then certainly the ability to deliver transformational brand ideas which can form the centre of gravity of a client's entire communications programme. Execution is the easy part: the big idea is the hard part. So the definition of creativity in agencies must be broadened. *The agency team must reform with a common purpose to create ideas that transcend advertising – then retreat to craft skills to optimise the outputs.*

Planning can continue to represent objectively the consumer on the agency team and can continue to bring research to bear on decision-making. The ability to be objective is entirely consistent with the ability to 'create' if the 'hypothesis testing' model of creativity is used.

Also, if the planner's job is to ask better questions, then perhaps we can afford to delegate the successful, sensitive and constructive answering of those questions to a highly skilled research industry, both quantitative and qualitative. What we should ask of them, though, is that they don't collude in throwing away 30 years of enlightenment; that we collaborate on new models and new measurements for communication's value, effectiveness and contribution. That we continue to believe in the creative imperative – perhaps more than ever.

Perhaps a new model for planning would not look so different from the old one. Perhaps many of us have started to practise it already. *In any case there is no question that the future for planning is every bit as exciting, and every bit as challenging, as its past.*

2 The role for advertising

Simon Clemmow

Introduction

Identifying and defining the role for advertising is the most important part of the planning process, and the one most demanding of a planner's skills. There are two key
reasons for this. First, because today's three converging mega-trends of consumer,
retailer and – above all – media sophistication mean that advertising no longer has a
'given' role in marketing communications. These days, getting 'upstream' into the
client's business, really understanding brands, and knowing the strengths and weaknesses of all available communications channels, are essential abilities of a good planner,
because a role for advertising can only be identified from the right vantage point.

Second, because the role for advertising is the starting point for all that follows. If it
is ill-defined – left ambiguous, inaccurate or unclear – then there are no solid foundations for developing advertising strategy or execution. Neither is there a basis for
meaningful research or evaluation. In fact, it's worse than that, because there's a negative multiplier effect. Ten per cent off on role for advertising might mean a further ten per
cent off on targeting which might mean a further ten per cent off on proposition, and so
on. So by the time you're looking at the finished advertising, it's got only a 50 per cent
chance of meeting its objectives! No – get it right at the outset.

This chapter shows how the role for advertising, properly identified and defined,
stands as a clear 'stake in the ground' in the whole development process.

Gaining the right vantage point

Agencies today can no longer say 'The answer's advertising, now what's the question?',
and clients are increasingly asking 'Is the answer advertising?'. For a start, their consumers are more sophisticated, vigilant and confident than ever before. They are
displaying heightened value sensitivity, demanding both genuine quality and competitive prices. They are not just advertising-literate these days, they are marketing and
brand literate. They are no longer a soft touch for the gloss of advertising. They are going
deeper into brands' components of authority – or 'core assets' – and will emerge with
their wallets and purses closed if they don't like what they find.

Retailers are exploiting this consumer trend by developing own-label away from the cheap generic alternative to the fully-fledged added-value substitute, investing in things like product sourcing and packaging design to take on manufacturers at their own game. So the answer for brand owners could mean that a product or packaging improvement, or a distribution or pricing change – or indeed a whole review of their *modus operandi!* – has a higher priority than advertising.

In parallel with these consumer and retail trends there's a media trend. People are consuming an increasingly varied and segmented selection of media; they are using 'on-demand' technologies to shape much more strongly what they see, and when; and new media vehicles are fast emerging, such as interactive television and the Internet. So there is an increasing number of ways clients can communicate with their consumers, and advertising isn't necessarily one of them.

Gone are the days when marketers could focus on network television advertising, secure in the knowledge that the finished film would both hit the vast majority of their target audience and represent the most effective medium for doing so. We can no longer assume that just because we advertised last year we should advertise this year, or that because there's a communications budget there's an advertising budget. Indeed, power is shifting away from advertising strategists to media strategists as decision-making moves upstream into clients' business planning meetings.

These days 'branding' and 'brand communications' are on the boardroom agenda for clients, seen as investments alongside plant and people that have to be justified and accounted for. And communication no longer automatically involves advertising agencies. It's the territory of management consultants, media independents, even design consultancies. The good news for ad agencies is that no one can yet claim the role of media strategist with credibility. No one can yet take a communications budget and carve it up with total knowledge and conviction in the face of the new 'channel blizzard' that includes PR, product placement, programme production, direct marketing, environment marketing, interactive marketing, relationship marketing, lifetime marketing, loyalty marketing, below-the-line, through-the-line, above-the-line and – oh yes – advertising.

Complacent ad agencies and planners beware! You may not even get the chance to identify a role for advertising – the decision may have been made to promote the brand on PR and direct marketing alone before you get into the room! The good news is that your discipline makes you well placed to at least take part in the debate. Get stuck in!

▌dentifying a role for advertising

What can advertising do well, and what is it not so good at? The truth is that it's impossible to match, with any precise science, communications objectives with the 'best' channel for achieving those objectives. Even case studies which have won IPA Advertising Effectiveness Awards aren't very convincing on this point. They're generally good at demonstrating how advertising helped meet the communications and business objectives set, rigorously eliminating other variables such as marketing mix adjustment and competitive activity, thereby 'proving' the contribution that advertising made. They're not so good at justifying 'why advertising' before the event, rather than another means of communication.

However, the large body of work published under the title 'Advertising Works' (Duckworth, 1981–97) does allow us to make some broad observations on the types of communication task to which advertising seems particularly suited (see Figure 2.1).

First, there is a plethora of case studies in which advertising is used in the almost 'classic' sense of delivering a consistent, 'added value' message on behalf of a brand, lifting an everyday product out of the ordinary. Perhaps not surprisingly, the examples are most

---

1. **Adding value to lift everyday products out of the ordinary:**

Walkers (1996)	Murphy's (1996)	Gold Blend (1996)
Philadelphia (1996)	Stella Artois (1996)	PG Tips (1990)
Peperami (1994)	Boddingtons (1994)	
Oxo (1992)	John Smith's (1994)	

2. **Building emotional brand values over and above a rational proposition:**

Levi's (1992)	BMW (1994)
Nike	Barclaycard (1996)

3. **Spreading new news quickly and widely:**

Daewoo (1996)	Direct Line (1992)

4. **Putting on public display a relatively discrete product:**

Wonderbra (1994)	The Economist (1992)

5. **Providing a corporate flag to salute and a public agenda to live up to:**

British Airways (1994)	Safeway (1996)

6. **Achieving broadscale targeting and mass social engineering:**

BT (1996)	National Lottery (1996)

(Date refers to year of winning IPA Advertising Effectiveness Award)

Figure 2.1: Roles for communication that advertising can perform best

prevalent in the food and drink categories. In food, Walkers Crisps, Philadelphia Cream Cheese, Peperami Snacks and Oxo Cubes show how advertising can be used to build a strong and lasting bond with a brand's public, fuelling growth and resisting competitive and own-label threat. In drink, campaigns for Murphy's Stout, Stella Artois Lager and Boddingtons and John Smith's Bitter in beer, the Gold Blend soap opera in coffee and the PG Tips chimps in tea have helped these brands rise above their scores of competitors.

Second, advertising is clearly useful when the communications objectives require the building of emotional 'brand values' as well as the delivery of a rational 'proposition'. The clothing category is an obvious area (brands like Levi's and Nike), but brands in other categories have benefited in this way too, from properties like BMW's 'ultimate driving machine' in cars to Barclaycard's bumbling secret agent, played by Rowan Atkinson, in financial services.

Third, advertising is good at spreading 'new news' quickly and widely. Daewoo cars (cutting out the dealer) and Direct Line financial services (cutting out the broker) are examples of this.

Fourth, advertising can benefit a brand enormously by putting on public display products that have relatively discrete target audiences. The poster medium is particularly suited to this 'propaganda' role, as case studies for Wonderbra and *The Economist* demonstrate.

Fifth, advertising is particularly useful when a company's communication needs to serve as a catalyst, or agenda setter, for its entire *modus operandi*. British Airway's self-styling as 'the world's favourite airline' is probably the most famous example, and Safeway developed creches, mother-and-baby parking places and baby changing-rooms on the back of its child-friendly strategy personified by its advertising property, the toddler Harry.

And finally, it seems that you can't beat good old-fashioned high-spend television and multi-media advertising campaigns when it comes to the need to talk to all of the people all of the time. BT has reaped the rewards of using advertising in this way, and the launch of the National Lottery provides another example of advertising's role in mass social engineering.

Defining the role for advertising

Having identified that there is a role for advertising, the next problem is defining what that role is. The difficulty here is that it depends on the context. At its most obvious, the role for advertising is simple: to communicate the proposition to the target audience in the right tone of voice! (This is true, but a cop-out. It may be the role *of* a particular piece of advertising in the context of a creative brief, but the role *for* advertising needs to take account of broader issues to make a compelling and directional case.)

At the other extreme, advertising has a role to play 'beyond the strategy'. For example, the brand might benefit simply from the status of 'being advertised', or being 'TV advertised'. Or it might benefit from the way it is advertised: being the first brand in its category to use posters, or a famous person, or a tone that doesn't talk down to its audience. These are all functions that advertising can usefully perform in the context of brand marketing, but they are pleasant side-effects rather than the main kick and lead to confusion between advertising and marketing objectives. (Statements like 'to put sales up', 'increase awareness', 'change attitudes' or 'recruit new users' are valid but bland within the context of an advertising strategy.)

The role for advertising has to find the middle ground. It has to both draw from the marketing plan and look ahead to the creative brief. It has to represent the advertising strategy in a nutshell: it must indicate what we wish to achieve with advertising, how we expect to achieve that aim, and even who our target audience is. It therefore lies at the heart of the planner's craft, and is the ultimate expression of the planner's ability to distil complex issues down to their essence. To get there, we have to start at the beginning.

Establishing the status of the brand

Where are we now? And why are we there? Many papers and books have been written on answering just the first two of JWT's famous ' Five Questions' which frame the planning cycle (King, 1977). (The other three are: Where could we be? How could we get there? And are we getting there?) Suffice it to say here that the answer to the first two falls into two parts: the status of the brand in the marketplace, and the status of the brand in the consumer's mind.

Both are vitally important, but the marketplace part is easier because information on things like market size and direction, seasonality and segmentation, purchasing profiles, penetration and frequency, brand and competitor share, distribution and pricing is generally more readily available, objective and reliable than more qualitative information on what's going on inside consumers' heads. Even so, it's important neither to pay lip-service to the data, nor to allow it to replace judgement, interpretation and intuition. For example, consumers may not define a 'market' in the same way a retail audit does; and 'macro' political, social and cultural trends may have more powerful implications for the future than the numbers show.

But it's the status of the brand in the consumer's mind that's the really tricky bit to wrestle to the ground in an insightful and inspiring way. Qualitative research can be useful here (although too much is done without sufficient regard for what we're trying to find out or who we're talking to). We can use it to ask questions about fairly rational, straightforward things like category buying and usage patterns, and brand selection and reputation, but its real value is that it enables us to investigate in depth motivations to use (and non-use) and where these motivations have come from – the associations and meanings a brand has, response to marketing and advertising activity, and so on.

A completed examination into the status of the brand can take any one of several forms, from a simple checklist to a full 'brand book', and no one form is likely to be appropriate for all brands in all markets. However, we have to start somewhere, and the principles are relevant to durables and services as well as fast-moving packaged goods, so here is a framework for our guidance (Figure 2.2). Use it as a reminder of the broad question areas that need answering and the relationship between them, and to give a systematic approach to your information search and a rationale for any research proposal arising.

Balancing ambition and achievability

Having established where we are and why, we need to take a view on where we could be, again in the market (in terms of, say, sales and share) and in the mind (in terms of positioning and personality). This ambition for the brand is based on business acumen and marketing expertise, and must be realistic given predicted 'macro' factors, competitive activity, and the client's attitude to investment, risk and return.

It is important to fully understand what our ambition is, and how it might be achieved. Are we looking for increased sales, or simply to halt a sales decline? Or are we looking to increase price and margin, thereby improving profitability? And does our ambition depend on gaining new users for the brand, increasing frequency amongst existing users, developing new usage methods or occasions, or what?

It's also important to be aware of the level of funds the client is prepared to put behind his ambition and over what period of time he is prepared to continue that investment. When will he be looking for results? Does he expect to see an effect in the short term, or is he prepared to adopt a longer-term perspective? It is clearly dangerous to advocate a particular role for advertising if the budget is likely to be insufficient to achieve the associated objectives.

Of course, where we want to be in the market must 'match' – even be a consequence of – where want to be in the mind. This is where the concepts of positioning and personality come in. Again, many papers and books have been written on both subjects, and it is not possible to describe or discuss them fully here. Essentially, positioning means owning a credible and profitable 'position' in the consumer's mind, either by getting there first, or by adopting a position relative to the competition, or by repositioning the competition.

Personality could be described as hard-sell positioning's soft-sell cousin. It is a metaphor for the brand's image and values, usually couched in 'If this brand were a person . . .' terms. Understanding and manipulating the concepts of positioning and personality are fundamental to a planner's skills. Get hold of two books called *Positioning: The Battle For Your Mind* (Ries and Trout, 1981; 1986) and *Understanding Brands* (Cowley, 1991; 1996), and read them. I do, again and again.

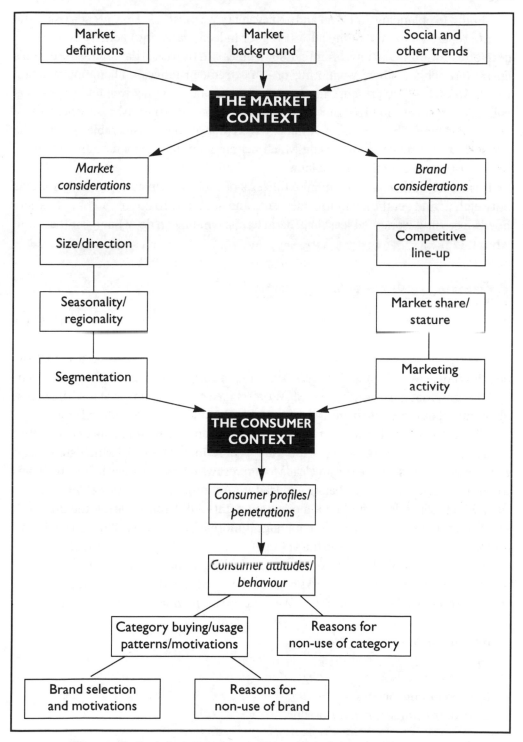

Figure 2.2: A framework to help establish the status of the brand

Finally, in balancing ambition and achievability we must ask 'How great a risk is the client prepared to accept?' Any advertising (or indeed marketing) activity designed to develop a new franchise for a brand can sometimes run the risk of damaging the brand's current franchise, either by 'ignoring' or – in extreme instances – 'alienating' existing users. And when you present the advertising proposals, you may well find a very nervous client trying to build reassurances for existing users into the advertising here, there and everywhere. The most likely result of which (apart from considerable aggro in the Creative Department) is advertising which neither stimulates new usership nor reassures existing users in their behaviour.

It is clearly important to minimise the level of such risk, ensure that likely returns outweigh it, and get the client to understand and accept it. To do so, you have to know how advertising works – at least in general terms: what it can do, what it can't do, and why.

Knowing how advertising works

After a century or so of formal study, we still do not know how advertising works! This isn't the admission of defeat it sounds; advertising is a craft, not a science, and asking how advertising works isn't like asking how a bicycle works – it's more like asking 'How does literature work?'! Nevertheless, it's very important to have a good grasp of the general theories that have been advanced and developed over the years, because they must all be part of our 'mental furniture' when we're defining the role for advertising.

'Classic' theories of how advertising works are mainly of the single-model kind; that is, 'The way advertising works is this way'. These include AIDA (which states that Awareness is necessary before and leads to Interest which is necessary before and leads to Desire which is necessary before and leads to Action); USP (Unique Selling Proposition, which depends on finding a motivating point-of-difference within the product); and Brand Image (which asserts that image is more important in selling a brand than any specific product feature, and that advertising works by 'adding value' to the *gestalt*).

However, as early as the 1930s it was acknowledged that advertising could work in more than one way, and frameworks began to be constructed. The most enduring from that time is James Webb Young's 'Five Ways' (1963), which says that advertising works:

1. By familiarising.
2. By reminding.
3. By spreading news.
4. By overcoming inertias.
5. By adding a value not in the product.

It is very easy to underestimate the value of these observations, and it wasn't until the 1970s that most of the theory was developed which underpins our thinking today.

Learning from the university of advertising

Thinkers and writers associated with JWT – and its sister market research company BMRB – have, over the last 30 years, justifiably earned that agency the accolade 'The University of Advertising'. Some seminal publications, all of which are worth getting hold of and reading (and all of which should be available from the IPA), are listed here (Figure 2.3). But they represent just the tip of the iceberg: our continued 'ignorance' about advertising is certainly not a function of the number of words written about it! For the purposes of this chapter I can do no more than scratch the surface, and guide the reader to useful references on the subject.

What Do We Know About How Advertising Works?
Timothy Joyce (JWT, 1967)

The Consumer Has a Mind As Well As a Stomach
Jeremy Bullmore (JWT, 1972)

How Advertising Works
John Treasure (JWT, 1973)

Repetitive Advertising and the Consumer
Andrew Ehrenberg (JWT, 1974)

Practical Progress From a Theory of Advertisements
Stephen King (Admap, October 1975)

Humanistic Advertising: A Holistic Cultural Perspective
Judie Lannon (JWT, 1983)

Over-Promise and Under-Delivery
John Philip Jones (JWT, 1991)

How Advertising Works: A Review of Current Thinking
Colin McDonald (ex-BMRB) (NTC, 1992)

Figure 2.3: Seminal thinking from 'The University of Advertising'

A good starting point is Timothy Joyce's 1967 paper, 'What Do We Know About How Advertising Works?'. It covers a lot of ground and is valuable because it provides a useful historical overview of alternative theories about 'how advertising works', neatly disposes of most of them, questions many previous assumptions about advertising and behaviour (for example, the validity of linear sequential models such as AIDA, and the premise that the consumer is a passive, rational receiver of information), and then makes some sensible conclusions regarding the roles that advertising can reasonably perform.

The basic tenor of the paper is best summarised in visual form (Figure 2.4). Adver-

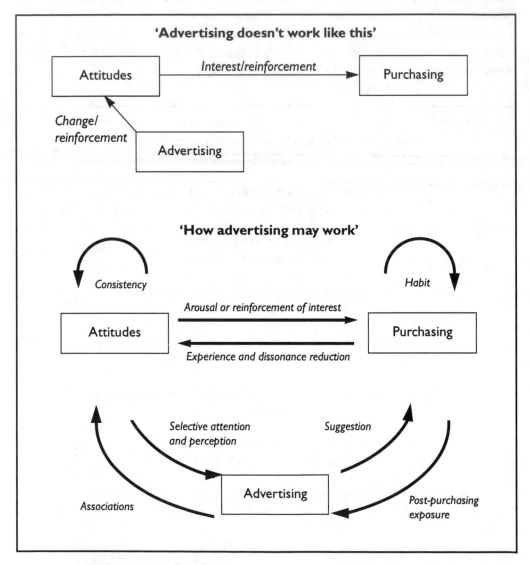

Figure 2.4: What we knew about how advertising works in 1967

tising doesn't work simply by changing or reinforcing attitudes, leading to interest in or reinforcement of a purchasing decision. Rather, advertising may work via a complex relationship of interacting variables: purchasing influences attitudes which in turn affect preconceptions to advertising, advertising can suggest purchase without the need for an intermediate variable, and purchase can heighten attention to advertising. In addition, there is a 'natural' consumer tendency towards consistent attitudes and purchasing habit irrespective of external stimuli – 'inertia' – which advertising always has to work with or against.

What's either reassuring or frightening – depending on how you look at it – is that when Timothy Joyce reviewed his work in 1991, there seemed little reason to change his basic conclusions, even in the light of the intervening 24 years of further development in advertising and research.

Of course, a lot of water has gone under the bridge since then, and a lot can be learned by taking a paddle – or even a swim! – in it. The biennial IPA Effectiveness Awards were established in 1980, so there are currently nine published volumes containing a total of 180 case histories which demonstrate that, properly used, advertising can make a measurable contribution to business success. In doing so, they foster a better understanding of the ways in which advertising works, and the introductions to the volumes – which highlight the lessons learned from the case histories therein – are required reading for any planner.

But it's back to JWT and the 1970s for my final model of 'How advertising works', and one which is particularly relevant to the construction of a framework to guide the planner in his definition of the role for advertising. Stephen King's 1975 paper 'Practical Progress From a Theory of Advertisements' constructs 'a scale of immediacy' in terms of the desired response to a particular piece of advertising (Figure 2.5). This scale starts with the simplistic view that advertising affects action directly, then modifies it on an increasingly indirect/less immediate continuum of intervening responses, from seeking information (perhaps by filling in a coupon or telephoning a number – the 'Tell me more' response) right through to reinforcing attitudes (the 'I always knew I was right' response).

In between there are responses concerned with the receiver relating the brand to his own needs, wants, desires or motivations ('What a good idea'), recalling satisfactions and making short lists ('That reminds me') and modifying attitudes (the 'Really?' response). The great strength of this model is that it recognises that advertisements can differ in terms of either the speed or the complexity of intervening responses, or both.

Conclusion: a planner's guide

So – what does all this mean as far as identifying and defining the role for advertising goes? I think I've made two basic points. The first is that identifying the role for advertising is a much more significant part of the planner's job than it used to be. Identifying the role for advertising within a client's total communications budget is now part of an upstream decision-making process which involves more senior people and interested parties than ever before. The days are fast approaching when media strategy will (in its very broadest sense) come before advertising strategy.

The second is that, having identified the role for advertising, defining it unambiguously, accurately and clearly is the ultimate expression of a planner's ability, because it represents the advertising strategy in a nutshell. It depends on having established the status of the brand, both in the market and in the mind, having balanced the client's ambition for the brand with his commitment to achieving it, and knowing 'how advertising works', both in general terms and how this piece of advertising is expected to work specifically.

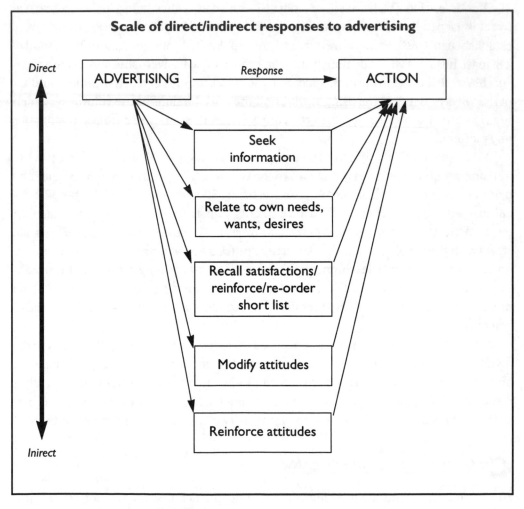

Figure 2.5: Stephen King's 'Scale of immediacy' (1975)

Remember, the role for advertising must indicate three things: what we wish to achieve, how we wish to achieve it, and who our target audience is. I leave you with a framework which provides 'scales of priority' for each of these three components (Figure 2.6). It excludes 'direct response' advertising, and the notation on each scale is given 'for instance' only, but as a planner you have to put your marker down somewhere, and the three components have to knit into a coherent whole.

For example, what are we trying to achieve (what are our advertising objectives)? Are we more up the 'awareness' end of the scale (perhaps with a new brand or a small brand) or are we more up the 'reinforce behaviour' end, with an established brand? The answer to this question will direct us towards who we are talking to (our target

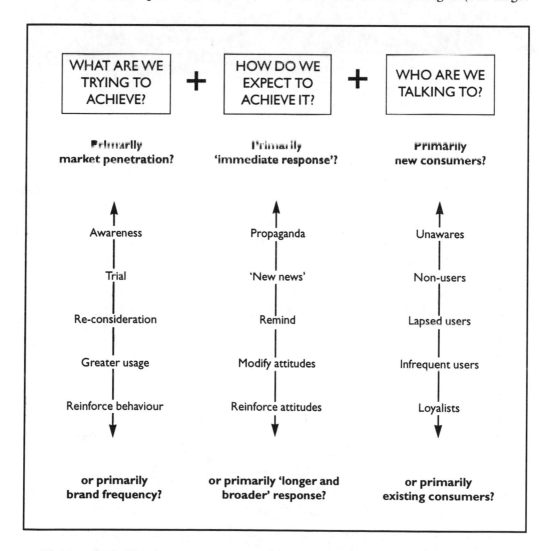

Figure 2.6: The three components of the role for advertising: 'Scales of priority'

audience). A 'trial' objective will obviously indicate 'non-users', while a 're-considera-tion' or 'greater usage' objective will indicate 'lapsed users' or 'infrequent users' respectively. And – coming full circle – our target audience must be in line with how we expect to achieve our objectives (our strategy). Whether it's via propaganda, 'new news', reminding, or modifying or reinforcing attitudes . . . but then – developing adver-tising strategy is a chapter in itself.

3 Developing advertising strategy

Leslie Butterfield

▌ntroduction: the brand doctors

The experience of working with and observing many talented strategic thinkers (mostly, but not always, Account Planners), has led me to the conclusion that there is, in the best ones, a highly developed sense of curiosity. I hesitate to call it innate, since I believe it can be honed and sharpened as a skill, though I suspect the kernel must be there at the outset.

When asked to distil this down to a single word that defines what makes a good planner, the word that is often used is detective. But whilst the detective analogy is one that suits the sequence of strategic development well, the *breadth* of approach that is required, the value of experience and the ability to marry analytical with imaginative skills all suggest to me that in fact the planner's role is more akin to that of a doctor, with the client as his or her 'patient'.

Consider the parallel for a moment. The doctor enters the patient's life at the point of consultation, usually at the patient's request. The patient is reporting one or more symptoms, and possibly volunteering explanations or even causes. But doctors draw a distinction between symptoms (as reported subjectively by the patient) and signs, i.e. things noted objectively by the doctor. The former may be misleading, the latter are indications of the true nature of the ailment. So, whilst listening carefully to the patient's reported symptoms, the doctor is also assessing the context of what is being reported: the patient's medical history, his or her demeanour in the consultation, the apparently irrelevant asides that may hold clues to causes (weight loss, dietary change and so on).

The doctor's task at this stage is simply to listen. Only after having done so fully does he or she move into proactive mode: probing for the presence of other symptoms that might give a clearer picture, looking for connections with other reported illnesses *historically*, constantly trying to narrow the field *retrospectively*, discarding the irrelevant, seeking to identify the key sign of the current reported condition; the 'problem' in other words. Only when this is defined does the doctor move *forward* to consider possible causes: cross-referencing combinations of symptoms and signs, running tests as an aid to his diagnosis. Having arrived at an identified ailment or disease, the next step is to consider possible treatments and the likely effect of these (the prognosis). Here too though he is checking for any intolerances, allergies or indications of resistance from the patient, a clue perhaps to rejection of the diagnosis or a lack of preparedness to collaborate in the treatment!

The good planner works along similar lines: listening carefully to his or her client, noting the unsaid as well as the spoken report, looking for the clues. Then probing for other explanations, clarification, more information, personal views.

The point of this analogy is that, just as with the investigation of an illness or ailment, the exploratory nature of the strategic process begins and ends at a very definite point. Whilst the planner (like the doctor) may enter the process some way down the line, his or her first task is to go back to the beginning and define the problem in the clearest possible terms. Only then can he or she start to broaden out the investigation of possible causes – possibly casting the net very wide. And then at some point comes the need for distillation as the planner moves into a more prescriptive mode: identifying and evaluating possible treatments as he or she starts to move towards a solution.

The search for strategy

As we investigate the sources of competitive opportunity, we will inevitably find ourselves talking more and more about the three-way relationship between the consumer, the brand and the advertising. This three-way relationship lies at the heart of our search, because the search for strategy has the same characteristics as the goal of strategy. And the goal of strategy is something like this (Figure 3.1):

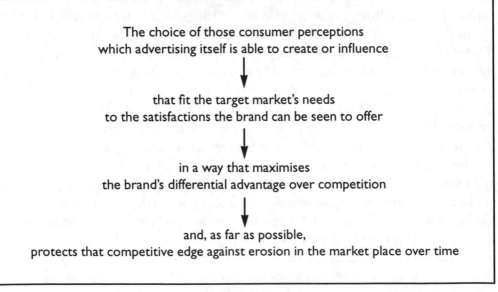

The choice of those consumer perceptions
which advertising itself is able to create or influence

↓

that fit the target market's needs
to the satisfactions the brand can be seen to offer

↓

in a way that maximises
the brand's differential advantage over competition

↓

and, as far as possible,
protects that competitive edge against erosion in the market place over time

Figure 3.1

And all this, of course, has to be achieved in a way that is compatible with the total marketing and corporate objectives for the brand.

One of the key reasons for setting advertising objectives is to clearly define the role which advertising can be expected to play within the total marketing context, and to ensure that this role for advertising is fully integrated with those for other marketing elements.

Second, it ensures that clients and agencies are aware of any assumptions that may be being made and hence are aware of the degrees of risk. By implication therefore it assists in determining advertising budgets.

Third, it helps the agency prepare and evaluate creative briefs and creative executions as well as aiding the decision about how best to monitor or measure the effectiveness of that advertising.

Given then that there are sound reasons for setting objectives, how should these be constructed?

Simply stated, the difference between objectives and strategy is as follows:

*   An *objective* is the goal or aim or end result that one is seeking to achieve.
*   A *strategy* is the means by which it is intended to achieve that goal or aim or end result.

The framework for strategic analysis is now beginning to take shape and I have characterised it for the purpose of this chapter as being in the shape of a diamond (Figure 3.2).

Diamonds are for ever

The diamond shape as a framework for strategic analysis is quite deliberate. The vertical 'dimension' approximates to the sequence of steps involved in the process (from top to bottom). The horizontal 'dimension' – the width of the diamond at various points, represents the breadth of consideration, analysis and research implicit in those steps. It does, as described above, start and finish as a point. But it does also 'cast the net wide' towards the middle of the process. It moves from the specific to the general, and then back to the specific again.

The larger part of this chapter will be given over to an exploration of the sequence outlined in this framework, with attention being paid to the appropriate actions at each step.

Defining the business problem

From all that has gone before it should be clear that whilst every advertising problem starts life as a business problem, not every business problem ends up with an advertising solution.

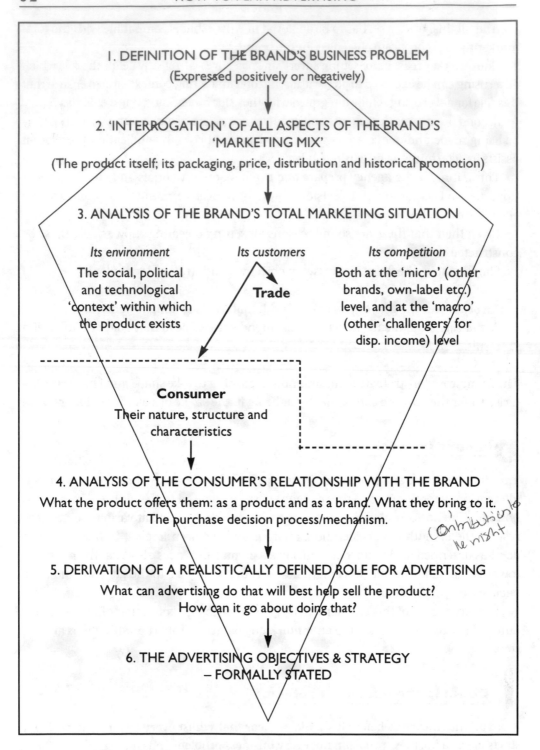

1. DEFINITION OF THE BRAND'S BUSINESS PROBLEM
(Expressed positively or negatively)

2. 'INTERROGATION' OF ALL ASPECTS OF THE BRAND'S
'MARKETING MIX'
(The product itself; its packaging, price, distribution and historical promotion)

3. ANALYSIS OF THE BRAND'S TOTAL MARKETING SITUATION

Its environment
The social, political
and technological
'context' within which
the product exists

Its customers
Trade

Its competition
Both at the 'micro' (other
brands, own-label etc.)
level, and at the 'macro'
(other 'challengers' for
disp. income) level

Consumer
Their nature, structure and
characteristics

4. ANALYSIS OF THE CONSUMER'S RELATIONSHIP WITH THE BRAND
What the product offers them: as a product and as a brand. What they bring to it.
The purchase decision process/mechanism.

Contribution to the night

5. DERIVATION OF A REALISTICALLY DEFINED ROLE FOR ADVERTISING
What can advertising do that will best help sell the product?
How can it go about doing that?

6. THE ADVERTISING OBJECTIVES & STRATEGY
– FORMALLY STATED

Figure 3.2: A conceptual framework for strategic analysis

To understand whether advertising has a role to play and what that role is though depends on clarity of definition at this early stage. Indeed it is generally true to say that the better defined the *business* problem, the quicker and more accurate the solution. And let's also be clear that we're talking about the brand's business problem, usually expressed in commercial terms, not just an attitudinal or 'image' issue. There must be a business reason why the client is talking to the agency. It is your job as planner to find it.

It may be there clearly stated in the brief, or apparent by reading between the lines. It may emerge in conversation or simply through observing some basic fact about the market. More usually though it will be shrouded: reported in the form of symptoms or observations, some accurate, some misleading, some perhaps irrelevant.

So the problem will need searching for: from available information sources, amongst industry or audit data or as a result of qualitative or quantitative research of your own. Just as importantly it may be defined either negatively ('true' problems) or positively ('opportunity' problems).

But however you arrive at it, arrive there you must, because without being able accurately to define the business problem you won't even be able to begin to set off down the road to an advertising solution, if that is indeed the outcome.

Let's take an example, one that we will use to illustrate this process. Some years ago within the portfolio of branded spirits of Seagram (UK) Ltd (one of the world's biggest drinks companies), one profitable brand (White Satin Gin) was underperforming in sales terms relative to others in the Seagram portfolio, and the gin category in total. In discussion with its recently appointed advertising agency, Seagram presented the problem exactly in this way, and suggested advertising as a possible solution. Resisting the temptation to 'just do it', the agency planner began to probe a bit further. Why was White Satin underperforming? Why did it use to perform better? What had changed about the brand? Or in the market?

After much investigation it became clear that the problem was not a general 'underperformance' one, but something much more precise. Whilst the spirits market had been generally static, the gin category had actually experienced some growth in previous years, largely because of its popularity at Christmas. White Satin, however, had consistently lost out in the important pre-Christmas period – *its otherwise healthy year-round brand share pattern declining markedly in the last quarter of the year.*

It should be apparent that this re-definition of the problem was a major step forward. Rather than a general observation of sales performance versus other brands in the client's portfolio or against the category in total we now had a much more precise understanding of when the White Satin brand was 'underperforming'. This then was our start point.

2 Interrogating the marketing mix

The concept of the marketing mix is one of the most basic marketing concepts of all – but still one of the most useful – if only because it stops us thinking that 'advertising is all', because in fact advertising is only *one quarter of one quarter* of the total mix.

Before we can define what role advertising can play we have to understand all the other components of the mix for our brand, and how they interrelate – hence the notion of 'interrogation'.

Let's look briefly at each element in turn.

Distribution

The key question here is: What role can distribution play in solving our 'business problem'? If we take our earlier example, it may be the case that our brand might not be well enough represented in those outlets used by occasional category buyers who only enter the market in the pre-Christmas period, like grocery multiples for instance. Curing that problem might of itself be enough to solve the share problem.

Pricing

Thinking back again to our White Satin problem, it might be the case that some sort of pre-Christmas price promotion would be beneficial, perhaps tied in with our attempt to open up new distribution channels. Or might this sort of activity simply aggravate the very problem that we have?

Perhaps it is *because* the product is thought too cheap for a Christmas gift that it suffers at this time of year. So should we *increase* the price, and if we do, what will be the effect in the other nine months of the year?

Product

Maybe there's something about the product itself that is aggravating our 'problem'.

Are the values or images that the product itself conveys somehow less appropriate to Christmas or 'gift-giving' than other brands?

If so, is *that* something advertising can address, or is it the case that these are harder to resolve and therefore we should be looking for a second (more seasonal) brand in this category?

Promotion

I've already mentioned price promotion, but is there some other way we can use one of the other below-the-line tools to advantage in this period?

- Could we offer some additional incentive related to our product?
- Does the product need *merchandising* better? Perhaps linked to some other *category* of product altogether?
- What do we know about how promotions work in this market?

The list is extensive, but the point is that there are many, many more ways to address a business problem than simply to say 'Let's advertise'. Too often that is precisely the knee jerk response that clients do get from agencies – and too often it's wrong. What I am trying to illustrate at this stage is that, as a planner, your perspective has to be broader than this if you are to gain your client's confidence – and indeed perform professionally yourselves. The 'mix' concept has to work as an attitude too: the planner needs to balance the various elements and opportunities that present themselves before moving on to a prognosis. So take a step back the next time you are in this situation: interrogate the product, and take a long, hard look at all those other aspects of the marketing mix that just might do the job better than a 30-second commercial!

3 Analysing the brand's total marketing situation

The analysis of the marketing mix, whilst valuable, has the potential downside of leading to a somewhat static view. So now there is a need for the planner to broaden the perspective further, to look over the horizon to the bringers of change, the sources of threat or opportunity at both the 'environmental' and 'competitive' level. This is important if the planner is to talk not only about 'what is', but also 'what might be'.

The environmental level is external to the product field in which we are involved. It embraces all those factors of technological, social or legal/ political change which can dramatically alter the shape and character of a market and our ability to survive in it. The competitive level is within the product field, taking a longer-term view of the marketing mix and the way it is likely to change and develop.

At the environmental level of technological, social or political/legal change, the contemporary marketplace furnishes a number of examples of astonishing range and power. I just want to take one illustration of each:

Technological change

In 1987 mobile phones were a rarity and a luxury. They weighed as much as a bag of sugar and were almost as bulky. Discreet usage was well-nigh impossible, hence the conspicuous 'yuppie' image that they developed. Ten years later, weight, size and price have all reduced dramatically – and penetration has increased correspondingly. There is now a strong repeat purchase market – and most first-time buyers are now social, rather than business users. Four networks currently compete for airtime sales, and soon the products will be the size of a matchbox, and only slightly heavier. Today you can wear a phone, not carry one. The effect of this development on the domestic phone is only just beginning. Soon, consumers will be choosing between conventional land lines for the home and, on the other hand, digital personal communications networks as their primary means of communication.

The effect of this blurring between the edges of conventional and mobile telephony will be to increase the importance of brands, as increasingly bewildered consumers look to this very traditional form of reassurance in an uncertain marketplace. This is the challenge that a brand like Motorola, for example, faces. The task of advertising will become polarised between short-term launch support for products that will lose their competitive advantage very quickly, or long-term corporate support which is designed to underpin the masterbrand and the company's reputation in its prime markets. This polarisation in the roles for advertising is something we shall be seeing a lot more of in the future in other product fields.

Visual 3.1:
Motorola press ad

Social trends

Social trends may be equally powerful in their effect on consumers, but without affecting the structure or economics of the marketplace in quite such a radical way.

Healthy eating is a trend of this type. Health is not a new preoccupation, but today's health concerns have outpaced the 'subsistence' issues that concerned earlier generations. The increase in interest seems to be almost exponential and is rich in threats as well as opportunity. The rise of brown bread and stoneground flour was an early harbinger. Red meats now have more to fear than just the threat from chicken. Butter sales are still going down and dairy fat brands have had to extend their umbrella to half fat products. We have all been long aware of these trends but threats and/or opportunities can still arise with what seems remarkable suddenness, witness the recent BSE controversy.

Social trends in health, fitness and environmental protection and so on have a number of characteristics which we can learn to recognise in our search for strategy. Most obviously they introduce new motivations which we can pick off with a new brand or sub-brand, or allow us to change the agenda for an old one. The many reincarnations of Lucozade are a classic example of this latter approach.

Political/legal change

Political or legal changes like those in technology can often affect the structure of markets, witness the enormous extra power handed to the big retailers by the abolition (in 1995) of retail price maintenance on books. Something similar has been happening with the progressive deregulation of financial services offered by banks, building societies and life assurance companies. Now that companies are competing in each other's markets (and must indeed do so if they are to survive profitably) marketing has to mean more than training the counter staff to treat customers decently, and advertising has to mean more than giving a human face to institutions competing for unsophisticated first-time account holders.

Consequently, there has been a change in the role and prime targets of media advertising, which in some cases quite rightly must now play second fiddle to direct marketing. But second fiddle does not mean unimportant. The enhancement effect of brand advertising on counter staff selling or on response levels from direct marketing or other promotional activities when there is a support campaign in the media, is becoming increasingly important and increasingly well understood.

Staying abreast of these environmental changes is itself a challenge, as the speed of change accelerates.

That said, the attitude of curiosity that I mentioned at the outset will hopefully give the planner a head-start in this quest. And as change accelerates, so too do the sources of information available to monitor it. Apart from the obvious 'journalistic' sources, there now exist increasingly accessible (and good value) on-line information sources such as FT Profiles and Textline, plus the now-ubiquitous Internet as a referencing opportunity.

What such sources mean is that whilst few can claim total ongoing expertise in a particular category, none can feign ignorance either! Within hours (or perhaps minutes) it is now easy to appraise oneself of the key trends, drivers and events within a given marketplace in a way that would have been impossible a decade ago.

In 1990, the Co-operative Bank was a little-known and even less well understood minority player in both the current account and credit card markets. It was also making losses.

My agency (BDDH) was appointed by the Bank in that year, and has worked with them subsequently to develop a unique proposition: that of the 'ethical' bank.

This positioning did not appear from the ether. It was carefully honed from a study of the Bank's history and working practices, its customer base and commercial ambitions, and above all from the desire to distinguish itself in a crowded market.

Over the years 1990–96, the positioning has been refined and developed – and expressed consistently in advertising – to the point where the Co-operative Bank has now shrugged off its former dowdy, 'cloth-cap' image and emerged as a desirable alternative brand that today even has a degree of cache with some audiences.

The commercial implications of this transition have been equally profound. Not only has the Bank significantly grown its share of current account business (specifically amongst younger, more upmarket customers), but it has also created for itself a platform for the successful launch of new products. Most notable amongst these has been the Gold Visa Card (a product that it would have been hard to imagine coming from the Co-operative Bank even five years previously), that is now the most successful and widely circulated Gold Visa card in Europe.

The brand campaign has not only successfully underpinned launches such as this – it has also transformed the internal morale of the organisation both at management and counter staff levels.

And in 1996, the Co-operative Bank made record pre-tax profits for the third consecutive year of £45m.

Figure 3.3: Mini-case: The Co-operative Bank

At the competitive level, it is worth bearing in mind that marketing and advertising are essentially competitive businesses even when the competition is not someone else's brand or service but a state of mind like ignorance or apathy. That said, there is no doubt that the planner has an easier task when the competition can be identified in specific behavioural terms like alternative brand usage. If you can answer the question 'What is who buying or doing instead? And why?' you've got a head start in differentiating both the problem and its solution.

In pursuing the specifics of advantage it is often best to start not only with what you know of the consumer's perception of what the brand does in the marketplace but also with what the client thinks it is doing. How does he see the marketing task? His and the consumer's view may or may not be the same, and if they are different there is a need to sell him the problem before you sell him the solution.

So what does he think is its differential advantage? What does he think he is selling, precisely, that the others haven't got? At its simplest this can be represented as some basic permutation of price and quality like:

- a better product at a parity price;
- a parity product at a cheaper price;
- a better product at a premium price;
- or a parity product at a parity price.

Asking oneself these elementary questions about what the client really thinks he's doing can be a powerful simplifier of the search for specific differences even though the answers are not always as black and white as the questions. In practical terms, a lot turns on what 'better', in this context, precisely means and here the list of possibilities is *not* mutually exclusive:

- better functional performance;
- better social gratification;
- better identity/personality.

The power of these simple distinctions gets blunted because clients and agencies have a tendency to believe, often without sufficient evidence, that what is supposed to be better is in fact perceived as such by the consumer! And, of course, there are some situations in which 'better' may simply mean 'different', that is to say better for some people some of the time.

Many clients and agencies tend to see performance strategies and gratification strategies as alternatives. But this isn't strictly true, even though as far as communications are concerned it may be best to be single-minded about one or the other. Generally, a gratification strategy in advertising will presume or imply better performance as well;

Nescafé Gold Blend would be a classic case in point. Their use of a 'soap opera' based around the developing relationship between two 'beautiful people' (and of course numerous coffee-drinking occasions!), suggested not only vicarious pleasure from those occasions, but was also laden with quality clues in the execution.

Visual 3.2:
Gold Blend TV still

Many brands (like Gold Blend) offer an enhancement of the role or situation in which they are consumed. Indeed, social gratification strategies are one of the most elegant and useful ways of differentiating the product benefit. They also happen to be heavily dependent on packaging and advertising in the marketing mix. In effect, both the packaging and the advertising say that this brand not only 'works better' but also 'means more', perhaps segmenting the market (by user or by end use) and justifying a premium price in the process.

Where better simply means 'different' we are in urgent need of the other classic source of differentiation, namely, the identity or personality of a brand. To look at some formats for creative briefs used in agencies you might have difficulty in deducing that this dimension of differential advantage even existed. And yet it is vital in many marketplaces: perfumes and standard lagers being prime examples.

4 An analysis of the consumer's relationship with the brand

As I have tried to indicate schematically in the Diamond illustration (Figure 3.1 above), an important and necessary precursor to this analysis is the understanding of the nature, structure and characteristics of the consumer.

Space precludes a full discussion here of the whole issue of targeting, i.e. how to go about defining the most appropriate audience for the activity being contemplated. It is

Retail brands are, in some respects, the most challenging brands of all from the point of view of strategy – because their physical realities at the local level are so varied.

Supermarkets though are something of an exception – all the major chains are now at some degree of parity, at least at the larger end of the scale.

Discrimination by consumers is increasingly based on the quality of the service offer and, of course, brand values.

Tesco and Sainsburys still have different identities, even though their larger stores are increasingly similar. My own client, Savacentre (part of Sainsburys), is the UK's leading hypermarket brand, but its identity is under-developed.

In qualitative research we used projective techniques to tease out these perceptions in a way that didn't force consumers to take up artificial positions based on their own shopping behaviour.

Instead we asked them to construct collages of photographic images of people and houses that represented their impressions of the competitive chains.

From this exercise, not only did we learn about the relative image strengths of brands like Waitrose, but also the extent to which Savacentre was described rationally rather than emotionally. Large houses, for example, were selected for both brands – but whilst in the case of Waitrose this reflected impressions of 'upmarketness', in the case of Savacentre it was to do with family

size and hence scale of weekly shop.

Very significantly, whilst the Waitrose collage was full of stereotypically 'posh' families, the Savacentre collage contained almost no human references at all (see collage board, left). A reflection of the lack of identity that the brand currently suffers from – and a significant challenge for BDDH in the future. (Watch this space!)

Figure 3.4: Mini-case: Savacentre

however worth pointing out a couple of 'golden rules'.

First, one of the classic 'pitfalls' is to confuse a definition of the target audience with a statement of the current customer profile. Available data sources will almost certainly yield the latter, but, unless the objective is solely repeat purchase, it is likely that the former will differ from this. It is here that investigation and imagination will need to go hand-in-hand in pursuit of this definition.

Second, it is increasingly unhelpful for a target audience definition to be couched purely in demographic terms. If others are to act on your strategy, then you need to give a qualitative feel as to how and why this target audience is appropriate, what triggers their behaviour, how they complement the current user profile, etc. Demographic indicators are useful in this, but can be very dry and depersonalised. Much richer are the insights that stem perhaps from an analysis of what other things these people do or buy, what their interests are, what role our brand might fill in their lives, what their feelings about our current communications are, etc.

These insights may often derive from qualitative research – but sometimes they may come from the intelligent use of quantitative sources such as TGI Lifestyle analysis or *ad hoc* segmentation studies.

Exploring and understanding consumers' relationships with brands is probably the most time-consuming, but most rewarding part of the whole strategic development process. And because it is by definition different for each and every brand analysed, it is also the hardest part of the process to be prescriptive about.

This is where the planner as researcher really comes into his or her own: designing and executing tailor-made research solutions aimed at gaining an in-depth understanding of the relationship. Qualitative research, in particular, has a key role to play here, and whilst it produces few genuine 'eureka' moments, it is almost always rich in the learning it provides.

It goes almost without saying that this part of the process is best approached with two things held firmly in mind. First, a set of hypotheses. It is poor practice indeed to, for example, approach a qualitative exercise purely on a 'Let's find out' basis. Rather the planner, perhaps because of the process that precedes this point, should have in mind his own thoughts about what the key dynamics of the relationship might be. This does not imply any lack of objectivity in the process, it is simply an extension of the Natural Science model into this part of the quest.

Second, for each project (and probably therefore for each focus group conducted within the project), the planner should have in mind 'the big question' that needs answering – which may be as simple as 'Why do people who buy this brand do so' or 'Why do those who don't, not'. It seems obvious, but too often researchers lose sight of this central ambition.

Finally, bear in mind that the issue here is *relationship*. For this reason merely reporting what consumers have said may not suffice. Much has been written on the value of projective techniques as mechanisms to elicit non-verbal representations of brand relationships and the planner most certainly admits these into evidence. Sometimes the truth of consumers' relationships with a brand is hard (or even embarrassing) to express consciously – and projective techniques provide a powerful cipher for emotional expression.

5 Deriving a realistic role for advertising

Perhaps this is a good moment to 'take stock' of what we have talked about thus far.

We started out by trying to define the business problem that the brand faced, and then examining or interrogating all aspects of the marketing mix in order to establish where advertising might fit in.

We broadened that still further by examining both the environmental and competitive environments in which the brand exists – and then analysed all aspects of the consumers' relationship with the brand.

The task now therefore is distillation, or if you like, synthesis. Out of all this knowledge and investigation we have got to pull out a direction, an intent and a way of getting there. But before we can even think about the niceties of objectives and strategics we must be crystal clear as to what role we are expecting advertising to play at all.

We can begin to define this role if we think back to some of the things that have been said so far. We know that our role of advertising must be defined with reference to the other elements in the 'marketing mix'; this has to be our first stage of distillation or synthesis.

There is no point in defining as a role for advertising some task that is more easily or cost effectively achieved through other means. (If the brand's entire business problem can be solved through improving its distribution base then that must be recognised, and the investment made towards that goal.) Hopefully, in addressing this first stage of synthesis it will have become clear that it is also not realistic to define the role of advertising as loosely as 'to increase sales'.

Our second stage of distillation lies in the concept of 'difference'. I have my own pet expressions in this area:

- 'Acceptable substitute'; and
- 'Desirable alternative'.

If what you think you can say about your brand only gets it as far as the former, then think again. To define the role of advertising as simply to make the brand 'acceptable' probably means you haven't gone far enough.

So here too is an opportunity for synthesis: does my strategy set me apart in any way from what others are doing, or could I easily substitute some other brand into my defined role?

There are very few 'Eureka' moments in strategy development. This though is one.

Clerical Medical appointed BDDH in 1989 to help them develop an advertising campaign in the newly de-regulated financial services market. The problems Clerical Medical faced were legion: small share, distrib-

uted indirectly (through IFA's) at a time when the market was increasingly moving towards direct contact, disparate product ranges (pensions, investments and life assurance), no clear brand positioning or history of advertising and a name that was not only dull but also misleading (they don't do medical insurance!).

In fact Clerical Medical had been set up in 1824 to look after the financial needs of clerics (the clergy) and doctors – two of the leading professions of that era.

Early exploratory qualitative research (at the time of the pitch) had been set up by the agency to examine the general attributes of companies in the sector. One of the techniques used in the research was that most basic of all: an adjective card sort exercise. As the cards, bearing single words like 'upmarket', 'friendly', 'secure', 'modern' etc., were being spread around the floor of the venue, one respondent leant forward and plucked a card bearing the word 'professional' from the array.

'That's interesting', he said, 'I've never thought of one of these companies catering for professionals.' (In fact, ironically, the card had originally been written to describe a company's *approach,* not its audience.) Nevertheless, this was indeed the 'blinding flash' – the groups that followed merely served to confirm the power of a strategic and creative route based on the idea of 'professional'.

All the pieces suddenly slotted into place: 'Professional' explained Clerical Medical's name and origins, it flattered and motivated the professional IFA intermediaries, and it (accurately) reflected the more upmarket bias of the company's product range and current customer base. More important still, interpreted in an inclusive way, it formed the basis of an advertising campaign based on the line 'The Choice of the Professional' that in turn was powerful and effective in bringing in new customers – particularly from the wealthier ABC1 segment.

Never in my experience has the power of a single word been so graphically demonstrated!

Figure 3.5: Mini-case: Clerical Medical

Defining the advertising objectives and strategy

Next comes the toughest part of all: distillation that springs uniquely out of the knowledge you have yourself gained in the course of your investigations and debate. I say it's the hardest because by definition each time it happens it is unique, but often absolutely vital. It may be the little 'kernel' of information that doesn't quite 'fit' with everything else you've read; the irritating little piece of data that somehow contradicts everything else you know about the brand.

You try and get round it this way and that, and can't. And then you realise why, and it begins to change the way you look at all that has gone before. And suddenly out of the whole morass of data that you've been buried in there emerges a new direction, that instantly allows you to discard 80 per cent of the rest of the knowledge you've gained because it's no longer relevant. When the 'blinding flash' hits you it suddenly clears up all the questions: the advertising objectives, the strategy, even the target audience.

Often though, the pursuit of these three elements:

* Objectives
* Strategy
* Audience

is much more tortuous: a combination of scientific method, detective work, common sense and intuition. But, once again, what all of them are about is distillation and synthesis.

Earlier we defined the difference between objectives and strategy as being:

* An *objective* is the goal or aim or end result that one is seeking to achieve.
* A *strategy* is the means by which it is intended to achieve that goal or aim or end result.

Given this distinction, it follows that one ought to be able to state an objective in the absolute, to preface it with the word 'To'. A strategy therefore becomes the conditional element, prefaced by the word 'By'. Hence a typical marketing objective might be:

'To increase market share for Brand X.'
and the marketing strategy might be:

'By continuing to improve product quality on the dimensions of taste and colour.'
Similarly a typical advertising objective might be:

'To demonstrate the versatility of Brand X.'
And the advertising strategy:

'By giving examples of both in-home and out-of-home usage.'
So, an objective is where you want to be, a strategy is how you intend to get there.

It should be clear from the example above and from the earlier discussion about setting advertising within a total marketing context that it is not appropriate to set objectives such as 'to increase market share' for advertising alone, since advertising alone is unlikely to achieve this. Advertising objectives should be set according to what advertising alone is capable of achieving and within the context of broader marketing objectives.

Thus, advertising objectives fall into a number of categories, generally relating to awareness, trial, informing or educating, changing attitudes, reminding, addressing image or identity or conveying a specific message.

From this it should be clear that objectives such as those relating to market share, penetration, sales, distribution or category growth are generally considered to be *marketing* rather than advertising objectives.

Overview and conclusions

If there is one big lesson from the process I've tried to outline in this chapter then it is this:

- Don't start thinking about advertising solutions first (the base of our diamond).
- Do go back to the beginning of the process, find out the essence of the business problem – and start from there.

Experience teaches good planners that the best defined business problems generally lead to the quickest and most appropriate advertising solutions.

But this maxim of: 'best defined, quickest solved' only works to the optimum if you know the right questions to ask, and have sufficient breadth of experience to interpret the answers accurately.

And this is where the medical analogy that I mentioned at the outset is so pertinent. In many respects, as we saw, the planner is like a doctor, and although the process is a great deal more time-consuming than the average doctor's consultation, the task of the planner is similar, and goes well beyond simply what the client says of himself.

Also as with modern medical practice, the planner's role is constantly evolving. Just as with the doctor, the emphasis is shifting from cure to prevention. Similarly, just as the doctor seeks to build trust and iterative learning into the relationship with the patient, so too with the planner. He or she seeks to add value to the relationship with the Client by building a databank of information and knowledge that can inform future decisions, especially where there are predictable, cyclical issues to address or where cumulative long-term understanding is vital.

And on this point of 'understanding', it is worth remembering that brands seldom exist in one dimension or have an immediately obvious 'truth' attached to them. That's why the good planner takes time to explore the brand in all its facets. He or she is a seeker after truth, because the truth is the most powerful weapon in the communications armoury. Given the choice between an invented virtue that can be bolted on to a product (commonly referred to as 'adding value') and a truth that already exists from which a powerful message can be derived (which can be likened to 'extracting value'), the choice should almost always be the latter.

There are many pitfalls on the way to that understanding. Common amongst these are the politics of the client (or even the agency) in terms of preconceptions about the brand. Then there are the 'myths' that build up around the brand that are often ill-informed or outdated (e.g., '70 per cent of our consumers are repeat buyers'). There is the classic trap of misleading research – that which may have been conducted amongst the wrong people and yet conclusions have been drawn which are then deemed to have general applicability.

The planner is not diverted by any of these! He or she does not take 'No' for an answer, but appraises each piece of research on its *own* merits, constructing hypotheses without fear or favour, seeking understanding against all these odds.

And when it is achieved, you can look back over the whole process with some considerable satisfaction, because your actions may have made a life-saving difference to the brand. But whilst you can feel rewarded, you can never feel complacent, because of one thing you can be assured: when the next problem comes along it's sure to be different!

4 Creative briefs and briefings

Charlie Robertson

Introduction

A creative brief should be brief, but it does not have to be creative. However, a creative briefing should inspire. The distinction between the brief and the briefing is often overlooked. Not making this simple division can lead to a lot of fruitless discussion. Creative briefing is a process, not just the issuing of a document. The writing of a brief forces the author(s) through a discipline which answers questions that otherwise may be left vaguely defined, or be left so open in the briefing of creative people as to hinder their grasp of the task.

Conversely, briefing is an expansive process where it is desirable that creative people can see a number of different routes made possible by the briefing. It is a time when thinking about the task should be allowed to roam free (albeit in a pre-defined direction, as advertising is a means to a sales end).

This chapter will address the most commonly asked questions surrounding creative briefs, and highlight some areas where developments are needed in the process. The focus of this chapter is on questions tabled by brief writers with an eye to the recipients in the creative department. It does not tackle issues arising from dealing with the marketers who instigate the need for the advertising process in the first place. It assumes the reader is relatively inexperienced in brief writing, or that the experienced reader seeks a refresher on the do's and don'ts of getting it right first time around. Some challenges to move the thinking on are tabled at the end.

An analogy is drawn which may explain why, amidst the toil, moil, and hurly-burly of real life in an agency, it sometimes feels that brief writing is a worthless exercise. You can expect to hear, if you have not already heard, these rejoinders: 'I never read it' and 'No one remembers the brief'.

It is not an uncommon dilemma that a written brief is perceived to reduce creative possibilities by boxing in thinking, despite its aim. This chapter hopes to be of help in relieving that tension.

The hurly-burliness of it all is broken down as follows:

1. The common questions.
2. How briefs are used.
3. The role of briefs in the creative process.
4. Component parts of briefs.
5. Where briefs go wrong.
6. Creative briefings.
7. Concluding remarks.

A few observations are made along the way based on working within different agency cultures, but the intention is to show the archetypal approach.

One thread to bear in mind through it all is that written briefs are an aid to good conversation where 'good' means 'clear, focused, and inspiring'.

The common questions

The hardy perennial questions of those setting out to write briefs are:

- 'Am I supposed to get it down to a single thought encapsulated in just one word?'
- 'Should the proposition be able to be run as a headline?'
- 'Is the proposition supposed to be like an endline for the campaign?'
- 'Should I talk to the creatives before I write it?'
- 'How is it different from just laying out what the client wants?'
- 'Who should write the brief?'
- 'Should I put lots of data in the brief?'
- 'Isn't it just about the proposition and the rest is padding because in the real world this is all the creatives look at?'

Before answering these questions you need to be very clear as to why you want to write a brief at all, and what role it plays for you in the strategic and creative processes in your own particular agency environment.

For example, agencies which have long-running campaigns seeking a new execution often argue that the brand and the idea of the advertising campaign are so well understood within the agency, that a conversation among the team around the table will suffice without any call for a written brief.

If the written brief in existence is correct, no new information is available on how the campaign works and no new market activity or restrictions impact on the brand's desired target market, it is hard to argue otherwise.

Assuming the wish is for a fresh start then thinking about the creative brief's role in the creative development process should help put a number of the common questions above in perspective.

2 How briefs are used

In seeking out a guide to best practice, we conducted a survey of a sample of a core target market for creative briefs with a creative department of 20 souls. We sought the answer to the question: What's the best brief you ever had?

We drew a blank. Not a sausage.

No one remembers the brief, but often people recall the briefing. So you have to wonder – why the fuss over a piece of paper, what does it matter, why not eschew written briefs, and can't advertising get written without this stage in the proceedings?

The vast majority of advertising does get written without a written brief; just look at the classifieds.

Working with different creatives

It struck me from my small-scale survey that the variety of desired ways of working were as numerous as the creatives we spoke to, and that different teams vary in what they want from a brief and how involved they wish to be in strategic discussions leading up to it.

'Just give me the proposition and nothing else and come back in 24 hours'

vs

'If I were you I would make sure that you talked to me before you let me read it.'

The common desire

You are expected to:

- turn the prosaic into the interesting;
- commit to a point of view;
- produce something simple, interesting, open;
- be single-minded but not too restricting.

This last point is slight paradox. The desire is for a focused point of view of the task, but not a prescription for an advertising idea.

Anchoring the mind

Following a briefing you should expect to hear and see drafts of work and ideas that are 'off brief' in the creative department. Changing the rules, moving the boundaries, shifting the goalposts comes with the territory. Briefs are not designed to, and neither will they, be likely to be followed slavishly.

The role of the brief amidst this part of the hurly-burly of real agency life is to anchor the mind.

After a while when revising work (and here again creatives differ in how they go about organising feedback on their work) the brief comes back into play in the reviewing of ideas, but first you have to have to write one.

3 The role of briefs in the creative process

A creative brief is the end of the strategic process, which is when they are usually written.

The briefing is a dialogue at the start of the creative process.

Different types of thinking and discipline are required along this path from the logical reductive analytical to the facilitation of good debate.

A creative brief is not 'the ad in longhand' but it is a statement of the problem irrefutably argued in words (this point will be revisited at point 7 – 'When words fail you').

It is a statement of purpose, most commonly whittled down to a one-page summary (archetypal layouts are within point 4).

A brief serves three masters

- The marketer should see an insightful summation of how communications strategy satisfies marketing objectives.
- The creatives should receive a clear focus of the problem which the advertising aims to address.
- The brief writer should benefit from going through the discipline of writing it by creating a succinct summary of his or her thinking about the strategy.

A written brief serves as a contract, treaty, or pact among its three masters.

Client cultures vary, but they all should approve briefs. Some clients you work with prefer briefs to be formally presented within strategy documents, while others prefer to see it in the form that the creative department will see it.

The nature of the contract

Achieving clarity of purpose cuts out the need for over-long meetings debating the nature of the problem.

You aim to encapsulate the orientation of the task, past, present, and future.

The brief acts as:

- *a point of reference* – benchmark of where we are coming from;
- *grist to the mill of thinking* – piece of stimulus using current information;
- *direction* – focused statement of intent.

A common misconception about the process of writing a brief, especially to a set agency *pro forma*, is that it creates straitjackets and cuts creative freedom.

The constant striving, quite rightly, to 'break the rules', or the argument that 'There are no rules for creativity' is not the same as having no boundaries. Canvases have frames.

Creative mindset

Two thoughts on the nature of creative thinking help illustrate this point:

> 'What characterises "creative thinking", apart from the intensity of interest in the problem, seems to me often the ability to break through the limits of the range – or to vary the range from which the less creative thinker selects his trials (of possible solutions to a problem). It is often the result of a culture clash, that is a clash between ideas, or frameworks of ideas. Such a clash may help us break through the ordinary bounds of our imagination. . . . But it seems to me that what is essential to "creative" or "inventive" thinking is a combination of intense interest in some problem (and a readiness to try again and again) with highly critical thinking.'
>
> *Unended Quest* (K.Popper, 1992)

> '. . . a certain amount of eccentricity, some excess, taint, or "tykeishness" is often prized by creative minds as a guarantee of ability to move apart or aside, outside. Drugs or alcohol are sometimes used to produce abnormal states to the same end of disrupting the habitual set of the mind, but they are of dubious value, apart from the dangers of addiction, since their action reduces judgement, and all the activities they provoke are hallucinatory rather than illuminating. What is needed is control and direction.'
>
> Introduction to *The Creative Process* (ed. B. Ghiselin, 1985)

So long as you bear in mind that you are trying to arrive at a well-reasoned dialogue, then tight creative briefs should really mean greater creative freedom, because they give direction and clearly frame the nature of the current problem that requires a new creative solution.

4 Component parts of briefs

The components of the 'contract' vary little from one agency to another, albeit with some different emphases.

In general, creative briefing formats in agencies are variations of a theme which address the very fundamental question of what aims to be sold, to whom, using what argumentation?

Many agencies aim for a single-page form and although some agencies eschew the written brief altogether the conversational debates should cover the same areas.

The general components

These are best tabled as questions to resolve.

* *Why* are you advertising at all; what are the objectives; what is advertising's role?
* *Who* is the advertising aiming to influence?
* *What* do you wish to communicate about this brand?
* *Why* do you think those it is aimed at will believe it?
* *How* do you wish to say it, what tone of voice?
* *What* do you think they will say having received this communication?
* What are you not allowed to convey about this product, or must be communicated legally within in paid-for communications?

The precise way the creative brief is composed can indicate how an agency believes advertising works by biasing the thinking as to where the focus of attention should be in the strategy.

Not all of the components above are addressed in every agency brief.

Agencies keep revisiting the area of how best to compose creative briefs in an endeavour to resolve the dilemma of how not to restrict creative freedom, but they are probably looking in the wrong place. Freeing up how you go about the process of strategic thinking from the outset is more likely to yield dividends than recomposing the format at the end of it.

Three archetypal formats, based on different agency *pro formas* are shown here.

Prompts are added to illustrate what writers should endeavour to achieve in composing a brief. The prompts differ between them merely to avoid repetition and can be transposed between them where the headings are similar.

The biases in these three examples are that Brief 1 opens on the advertising problem, Brief 2 on the customer, and Brief 3 on the client. The normal executional information common to the majority of briefs is shown only in Brief 3.

Good source material for studying briefs is the 'Creative planning – Outstanding advertising' series published by the APG in the UK as many of the cases contain the actual briefs which lead to successful campaigns. Some excerpts are used in the notes within the following three brief formats.

1. WHY ARE WE ADVERTISING ?

Surprisingly this fundamental question too often is poorly addressed.

e.g. consider two roles for the same product:

- using a single product line from a range as a flagship for overall consumer brand positioning is a different role to:
- selling more volume of the premier line in the range.

Watches brands tend to adopt this approach by featuring the best in the range to create prestige associations.

2. WHO ARE WE TALKING TO ?

Combine demographic primary target audience data and 'psychographic' profile – attitudes and outlook of typical potential user with highlights from qualitative research.

e.g. if the 'the early adopter' type was a potential buyer of the flagship of the range then the description would involve depicting their apirations, influences, current views of their choices in the sector.

3. WHAT MUST THE ADVERTISING SAY?

Concentrate on rational points of communication, competitive advantages and differences. Where these are lacking it forces you to focus solely on emotional aspects of your selling proposition (commented on in section 7 – 'When words fail you').

Why should anyone believe it?

Concentrate on evidence, hard facts, make sure the evidence directly supports your contention of what the advertising must say, e.g. British Airways bring 25 million people to other people all around the world every year.

This does not preclude you from some qualitative evidence such as associations with provenance.

VW, Audi and Porsche have all used their German engineering heritage at times in their brand positioning; beer advertising often uses provenance, e.g. Australian lagers and Irish stouts.

4. WHAT TONE OF VOICE?

Often the weakest part of the brief, as people find it hard to think of the variety of tones of voice one could adopt. Clichés include 'witty, confident and self-deprecating humour'; think of the brand character and personality (probably better terms for this area of the brief) and the advertising as a conversation with the audience. 'Mood and tone' is probably a better descriptor. A good example from British Airways brief in 1989 is

'Big, warm, emotional, goose pimples'.

5. WHAT PRACTICAL CONSIDERATIONS?

No point getting to here with all that build-up if you only have ten seconds of radio; be pragmatic.

Figure 4.1: Brief 1

I. WHO ARE WE AIMING THIS COMMUNICATION AT?

Pen portraits of individuals, e.g. the different attitudes toward products or services in question currently among users and non-users can help. We sometimes find it easier to describe a target type by describing who does not buy it and why, particularly for brands with 'inner directed' as opposed to 'outer directed' brand character.

2. WHY ARE WE PROMOTING IN THIS INSTANCE?

What is the precise role for the communication, e.g. are we trying to rectify a problem, impart news . . . ?

What role does Brand X play in their lives currently?

Do we wish this reinforced or changed?

What attitudes are we trying to change . . . ?

3. WHAT DO WE WANT PEOPLE TO THINK OR FEEL?

Often the clearest area of the brief in encapsulating the nature of task – the desired before and after effects. Consider what you hope they will ideally say, think, feel, do, having seen this communication. If there was a direct response, what would it be?

4. WHAT JUSTIFICATION ARE WE PROVIDING AS A SUPPORT?

What rationale is there to accept what we wish to say; what details do we think need to be communicated; what are the features, advantages, and benefits . . . of Brand X?

Existing work is often the main source of data; how has the campaign worked in the past?

Many great advertisements are based on a fact; what is surprising or different, what will interest creatives? The strangest information can be the best. Supporting evidence need not be points you wish communicated in the advertising but it can spark ideas, or be a starting point for creative thinking.

5. HOW IS THAT DIFFERENT TO OTHER BRANDS IN ITS FIELD?

Could anyone say what we wish to communicate or is it only true of Brand X?

6. HOW DOES THIS CONTRIBUTE TO BRAND X'S POSITIONING?

What aspects add to the perceived relationship with Brand X, differentiating it from Brand Y?

How do people really use/abuse the brand?

7. WHAT PRACTICAL CONSIDERATIONS ARE THERE?

e.g. legal restrictions on the advertising claims. This is usually seen as the most boring and restrictive part of the brief so do not put things here for the sake of it.

Figure 4.2: Brief 2

Job No	Date
Client	Product
Project	Media
Budget £	Copy/Air Date
Size/Time Length	

BACKGROUND *What has the client done before and how has it worked?*

TARGET AUDIENCE *Be specific. Try to give more than just socio-economic groups.*

OBJECTIVES *What does he realistically expect the ad to do?*

PROPOSITION *To persuade the target audience that . . . in no more than one sentence.*

SUPPORT *List any important information that backs up the main message.*

TONE *Accurately describe the desired tone of voice.*

DESIRED RESPONSE *Imagine a spontaneous quote.*

ATTITUDES *The more information about the consumer's preconceived ideas the better.*

MANDATORIES *Be sure it is mandatory.*

REQUIREMENT

Date issued	Account Director
Due date	Planning Director
Time allowance	Creative Director

Figure 4.3: Brief 3, with normal surrounding details for any brief

Some questions to ask of your brief:

Why advertise?
- Is there a clear agreed role for advertising?
- Is this realistic (can advertising/communication achieve it)?
- Is it appropriate?

Target audience:
- Does the brief explain why these people are the target?
- What insight or fresh information about them does it give?

What the advertising must say – the proposition:
- Does the proposition have meaning, truth, and promise?
- Is it single-minded?
- Is it supported or supportable?
- Does it clearly fit with the rest of the brief?

The proposition would be unlikely to make sense in isolation. A good brief will have interesting thoughts and will draw clear conclusions in each of its parts, which will explain why the proposition is how it is.

Support:
- What facts have you included to support your case?
- Two thoughts on ways of seeking good supporting evidence are:
  'Tell me 20 things I don't know about the product'
  'Interrogate the product until it yields its strengths'
  N.B. facts are not necessarily rational, e.g. it is a fact that cat owners love cats, but that is an emotional point.
- Are the facts you have included relevant to the proposition?
- Have you included *only* the relevant facts?
- Have you interpreted the facts to fit the 'story' the brief tells?

Restrictions:
- Are any restrictions you have in the brief really necessary? Who says?

Consistency and logic:
- Is it consistent?
- Do all the parts fit logically together?

Some general points on creative briefs

If the most interesting thoughts don't fit on the paper, save them for briefing. Perhaps you will have supplementary detailed reports that you think may be of interest to read to give more of a flavour for understanding the target market or the brand's history (sometimes referred to as the brand's *archaeology*).

Rational vs emotional:
- Competitive differences and distinctive features should be easy to ascertain and describe (if there are any).
- Brand character/personality/tone of voice/identity – the emotional parts of the equation are the hardest to capture in a written brief. Try to ascertain the underlying values associated with the brand.

Writing it:
- There is a danger of losing focus if you write by committee.
- The principle is one of responsibility – who will write it and subsequently defend the point of view? The person with most insight into the perceptions of the target market is usually best placed to write the brief, but seek a good scribe and those with a lively turn of phrase to make it vivid.

Language:
- Is the brief written in 'normal' language (avoiding jargon and marketing-speak)?
- Is the language clear and simple?

Forms and formats:
- The positive value in obliging to you to fill out boxes is that it forces you to think the problem through. The ultimate problem of formats is that, over time, familiarity can breed contempt, and the routine questions start to get routine answers. They help so long as it remains a questioning process focused on defining the problem and not used to force a finished pattern as a solution.
- In the writing of a brief, if the boxes don't help, then move them around (even if you have to move them back again), or reword them slightly e.g. 'mood and tone' is often easier to conceive than 'tone of voice'. A mistake some agency software designers have made is that the formats are typed top to bottom in sequence, restricting how you can cut, paste, and edit what you have typed. Most brief writers do not compose them sequentially, but rewrite them several times.

Involving creatives:
- It is hard to think what harm it can do in chatting about advertising problems with creatives early in the process. Often agencies do not allocate teams early enough to a

project to make the most of the early conversation. In our research, teams differed in their desire for early involvement, but judging the mood, understanding, and anticipation as early as you can is largely a good thing. It gives you ideas for your brief and a brief for your briefing to survey the target market. The best early conversations are when you have begun to form a hypothesis for discsussion.

The most important question
Have you committed yourself to a point of view ?

5 Where briefs go wrong

Borrowing from the idea that in order to write a good radio play, you should start by studying bad ones, perhaps you should consider that one way you can improve your creative brief writing is to learn about bad briefs and how to spot them. At worst they are lazy thinking, catch all descriptions of the problems, repetitively worded, contain wishful thinking about what advertising can achieve, and full of contradiction. There are often debates on semantics which distract you from achieving the aim of a well-reasoned dialogue (this point will be revisited at the end of this chapter 'When words fail you').

Most briefs suffer from some of these problems. Some briefs you read suffer from all of them.

It is hard to write a brief. Expect to make some of these mistakes but try to identify them and correct them before you brief the creatives, e.g. ask a colleague not on the account to read it cold to see what sense they make of it. There's nothing like the creative process to flush out a bad brief. Good training for brief writers is to try and write advertising from briefs. It at least generates an understanding the notion of staring at a blank piece of paper with insufficient inspiration, or a good frame of reference for what you are trying to achieve.

Common errors
However, sticking to the task in hand of merely writing the brief in the first place, here is a list of common errors to avoid:

Opposites – 'Not only but also':
* Briefs that include contradictions
  e.g. in brand character or tone of voice descriptions 'modern and traditional', 'contemporary and classic'. This usually displays a fear of change/genuine new thinking therefore evidences a desire to cling on to past.

Repetitive:
* Same point crops up everywhere, e.g. role of advertising is to 'create awareness of

new feature', proposition is 'communicate new feature', support is 'new feature is now available' etc.

Wishful thinking:
- run-away optimism not rooted in consumer data
  e.g. exaggerated claims like 'Brand x is more than just a car, it is the future here today'.

Lazy:
- generic, nothing unique or distinctive, could be for any brand in the sector.

Long:
- familiar or clichéd, often full of marketing words: beware 'quality', 'value', 'versatility'.

Catch all:
- the politician's brief that has something for everyone, which proves hard to disagree with because it is not selective with information, and does not take one clear point of view on the nature of the task.

6 Creative briefings

Your brief has been signed off. 'Job's done' thinks the unwary brief writer, whereas all you have achieved is being well prepared for a conversation.

Think of a picture of the twin-faced God Janus at this juncture: facing backwards is the strategic process you have come through. Creative briefing is facing forwards and deserves a fresh outlook. At the start of the creative process the role of your briefing is to spark ideas. Thinking about briefing and anticipating questions that will be asked is a good self-reviewing process that might force you to revise the brief. Have you thought about competitive brands' ideas? Does your brief contain or lead to ideas? How will it not just lead to the same ideas as competitive brands' advertsing?

The challenge for you is to inspire. This is where your input is most likely to be recalled.

Good briefing practice

Bearing in mind that different teams work in different ways you should tailor briefings to individuals/teams. In particular be sensitive to creative interests/worries, e.g. this is a boring category for advertising.

You have to invest time and energy in relationships with creatives, learn from them in order to be able to brief them better next time. Talk the right language, no jargon.

Appropriate language comes from discussing advertising ideas more than marketing strategy.

Preparation:
- Do not leave it until the last minute – preparation takes time.
- Consider who should be there, when, where, and how to conduct it.
  e.g. briefing beer advertising at breakfast may not be most inspired time, unless it was a German breakfast beer and that was the point of conducting it then.
- Do not be rule-bound – go beyond systems.

Mood and tone:
- The added value of briefing as opposed to just slipping the brief under the door and letting the creative team read it, is the spark of conversation. Start a dialogue. Conversation is the most powerful tool in making sure you get the best out of your team.
- Make the briefing fun, but make it relevant. You need both for best results. Be aware that your attitude to the task can be demotivating for creatives.

> You get (account) teams coming in here having spent three weeks working on a brief and they are bored with the brand's problems and you think what chance have we got if they can't think of anything interesting to say after this length of time?

- Demonstrate knowledge of the issues, drip-feed data if appropriate, but you do not have to be a walking encyclopaedia on the subject matter. Leave some things for later rather than shoehorn everything in. More questions will occur after a few days anyway. It is probably a measure of your success that the team will come back for more information later.
- Be ready to defend the brief, but do not die for it – remember the end is distinctive effective advertising.

Bring the brief to life:
- Who could help you?
  e.g. a tyre brand – a professional driver at a race track 'torture testing' .
- How could you do it?
  e.g. for a perfume brand – blindfold briefing to emphasise touch, taste or other sense and discuss image associations.
- Where?
  e.g. for beer – in the right type of pub for the target market.
- As stimulus for how you can add value to a briefing, beyond just discussing the brief, think of where a product is exposed to its toughest test as a way of demonstrating its capabilities and you might come up with something to exploit.

Risks:

• Being highly theatrical is not always appropriate, this is not an audience that tends to be easily impressed. Relevance is crucial: creatives will dismiss self-indulgence. Using well-known film clips as an example of tone and style may be good but acting it out in a home movie is probably inappropriate.

7 Concluding remarks

Three watchwords

Clarity:

• It is not an uncommon challenge to brief writers to be asked:
  'Would my mum understand it?'
  Given that many a mum is in the target market, this is not a facile remark so much as a healthy challenge to the clarity of the brief. When the mum in question is not in the agency do not be afraid to use anyone not connected to the account you are working on as a sounding board.
• A creative brief does not have to be creative.
  'If it has to be dull to be clear, give me dull'.

Brevity:

• A creative brief should be brief.
  'Give me an hour and I will speak for three; give me three weeks and I will speak for 15 minutes' (anon., attributed to a French politician).
• Edit out what you do not need, to make your point crystal clear.

Dialogue:

• The creative process needs fuel. Briefing is a process, not a one-off act; not a monologue, but an opportunity to bring the thinking to life, and be a stimulus for ideas. Ideas improve through dialogue and debate.

The planner's outlook

The aim is motivation of the creative team, your key target market. Planners can help by being inquisitive about the issues, persistent in analysing the problem, and sensitive to the creative process. A basic grasp of rocket science helps.

The match is the brief, the ignition is the inspiring dialogue and the flare is creative.

Matches get burnt and thrown away in the process, after which you get another match to ignite the next flare. Briefs that lead to long-lasting advertising campaigns are maybe the long-lasting taper.

When words fail you

Two trends put pressure on the approach outlined in this chapter.

International business and global brands:

- The market horizon of many brands is getting wider. Having intimated earlier in the chapter not to get bogged down in semantics you need to worry how well written briefs translate, and convey what you mean, when working with teams internationally.

'ESP':

- In a number of markets competitive points of product difference are narrowing, and the emphasis of differentiation is based on the notion of the 'emotional selling proposition'. Here again you have to worry about how well your words communicate the feelings and images that make the difference between brands, e.g. creative briefs for perfume brands.

   Visual briefs are an area worth developing your thinking about. Add a visual dictionary to the *OED* or *Websters* on your shelf for a start to help generate material to put together a collage depicting the desired brand imagery. The brief for this to yourself could be to show who uses the brand, how, where, when, to impress who, and what are the moods associated with the brand. You might start this with word and picture associations with the brand in your qualitative research. A collage of film clips is often better in encapsulating desired mood and tone for the brand as an aid in your briefing. Articulating feelings is hard. We often find it easier to depict images of what a brand is not. Your visual brief could compare and contrast what Brand x is and what it is not in terms of image associations.

Hurly-burly

There is moil and hurly-burly in real agency life with a great capacity to create confusion. Because of this, brief writing is worthwhile toil in creating an anchor for the mind. It helps you facilitate well-reasoned dialogue.

5 The requirements for creativity: a creative director's perspective

Jaspar Shelbourne and Merry Baskin

Introduction

Let's start with a quote from Stephen King, the JWT man responsible for all this account planning malarkey in the first place:

> 'People like James Webb Young, Rosser Reeves, David Ogilvy and Bill Bernbach were all superb planners.'

(The irony here, of course, lies in the fact that all these guys were exceptional creative people, veritable legends in their own lunchtime.)

Let's follow that up with a complimentary quote from one of today's top creatives (we won't reveal his name in case he gets big-headed):

> 'Planning is excellent when we all remember why we are doing this in the first place; collectively to produce great advertising which elicits the right response from the consumer.'

That really is the summation of what this chapter is all about: collaborative teamwork makes for better advertising, regardless of the discipline or department in which you work. The traditional relay race analogy of a linear advertising development process where the 'problem-solving' baton is passed first from the client to account management then to planning then to the creative department ending up with media, is becoming less and less applicable. Not only has the finishing tape for this metaphorical 'race' moved further down the track in terms of the distance we must now cover to meet our clients' needs, the race itself has evolved into a team chase, where the runners race together in parallel. This chapter therefore intends to talk less about the processes leading up to the advertising and more about the practical sharp end of actually creating it. Which is why this section has been co-authored – it may be the creative director's perspective, but he shared it with the planner first!

The areas we will cover are as follows:

1. How do creative people get ideas?
2. Why is it important to know your creative team?
3. What do creatives want from a brief?
4. What do creatives want from a briefing?
5. Follow-up time – what's needed?
6. What do creatives dislike about planners?
7. 'Ten Tips for Top Planning'.

How do creative people get ideas?

Albert Einstein would agree that knowledge is essential to good creative thinking and that this knowledge must be absorbed before it can re-emerge as a fresh idea. As long as there is a need for advertising, there will be a need for original yet relevant ideas and vivid expressions of them.

In order to come up with that fresh idea a creative team needs to be briefed.

How do creatives get an idea? The following iterative stages are an attempt to turn the crackling of static within our heads into a definable, recommended procedure (fat chance!).

- First, gather your information, both general and specific (or as Ron Collins of WCRS fame and Grace Slick of Jefferson Airplane used to observe, 'Feed your head'). Some art directors keep scrapbooks and paste in an interesting visual image or cutting that has struck them. They may not have a use for it right away, but will then thumb through these pictorial 'rolodexes' when in search of inspiration.
- Allow yourself to digest what you have gathered; seek out the interesting tid-bits that may lie within. Look at them from different angles, mull them over, play mental ping-pong with your art director or copywriter partner, who is able to add something and then send it back. You will know when you are onto something when it's easy, and things just start to fall into place. (This stage may continue until things make no sense at all.)
- Drop the subject, forget all about it, put the problem out of your mind and let your unconscious take over the incubation. Do something else that stimulates the imagination, like going to the movies or listening to music. Or even take a long lunch. (Some things never change – only who's paying.)
- Usually, out of nowhere, the 'Idea' will appear – Eureka!
  Here's an example: (see Storyboard 5.1)
  'When we were working on the Kit Kat brief that became the Pandas ad we realised that we had spent two days thinking too loose. We realised that we had to look at the structure, to think laterally about it. The traditional 'Have a break, have a Kit Kat' ads worked along the following lines: i) activity, ii) take a break, iii) activity with a spin. We looked at an alternative structure: no activity – activity – no activity, with the Kit Kat break taking place during

1.

2.

4.

5.

7.

8.

Storyboard 5.1: Kit Kat

3.

6.

9.

the activity. The pandas came in when we thought about those 'nothing happens' news stories, such as the world's press around a zoo enclosure waiting for the Giant Pandas just sent from China to come out and mate, only they never do. Understandable really. They've just travelled thousands of miles, it's nice and dark and warm in the straw in their cage. Why should they? This is a story that everyone is familiar with. It's the familiar pantomime device of 'Look out, he's behind you', but given a fresh twist. And it gave Kit Kat yet another classic commercial in a campaign that has been running since 1934.'

Later, take the idea out into the cold grey dawn of reality and re-examine it (probably the next day). Work on it to make it fit the practical exigencies of the brief. The idea may be fresh and original but it may also be unworkable. By 'unworkable' we mean impossible to execute, irresponsible, stupid, preposterously expensive, impractical or any or all of the above. Good ideas have self-expanding qualities. They also do not recognise their parents (as in the thought 'A good idea has many fathers'), and others who see it should then start to add to it. Show it to people you trust and discuss it with them, strengthen and nurture it before Herod (that bloke in the Bible that likes to murder other people's children, a.k.a. the client, the consumer, the account people or, heaven forbid, the account planner) arrives and starts trying to kill it. (One of the issues raised with the Kit Kat Panda script was 'Won't it make the brand synonymous with losers?' The answer is no, of course not, because we the audience know what's going on, he doesn't.)

The other thing to remember is that the generation of ideas is a very personal process, and each creative person tends to 'do it' differently; some approach it logically, needing to sit at a desk with a stack of perfectly sharp pencils and a pristine pad of A4 in front of them; others may do it more instinctively, preferring to sit in the bath, lie on the floor and gaze at the ceiling, etc.

2 Why is it important to know your creative team?

In the agency you will have several core team members working on a piece of business:

- The creative team comprising art director and copywriter.
- The account planner (we assume!).
- The account management group comprising tiers of account handlers.
- The media planner and buyer (in-house or independent).
- The production department (TV and print).

Like most things in advertising, it all comes down to the people as much as the process. An agency will have its own work practices, systems and culture, yet the working relationships between different account teams within the same agency will vary. Systems, protocols and forms can try to legislate for things to work smoothly, but the real lubrication comes from the way people work together. How well do you know the people in your team?

Given that the creative department is the most important department in an agency (we don't think you will find anyone to disagree with this assertion) the planner's relationship with his/her creative team is the most important one he/she will have. *The relationship between the planner and the creative team is as important as that between a copywriter and an art director.* It's also a variable thing, with some planners working very well with some teams but badly with others, or some teams expressing a preference for a particular planner and an aversion to another. So, how do we feel about each other?

Specifically, how well do you know your creative team? Do you know what work they have done that they are proud of? Do you know what makes them tick? Do you know how to get the best out of each other? Do you have respect for each other's skills? You should. As the planner, the catalyst or glue within the team, you are their conduit to the consumer, and, hopefully, the starting point for creativity. (You are also the one who is going to have to be the ultimate diplomat – persuading them to think differently about a brand they grew up with, or explaining why their idea bombed in consumer research but that it is still salvageable.)

The previous chapter has dealt with two key forms of communication within the agency: the creative brief and the creative briefing. Our advice, before you start working on what you know about the client, the product and the consumer is to think about the primary target audience for these media, the creative team, for whom the brief is written, and for whom the briefing is devised. How well do you know us?

3 What do creatives want from a brief?

In true planning style, the best way to get to know your target audience is to talk to them. So that's what we did. The quotes peppered throughout this chapter are verbatims from members of the 40 creative teams working at JWT, a disparate bunch of art directors and copywriters, each with their own experiences, preferences and creative methodologies.

> 'The real point here is that you try to think of an idea at any time of the day or night (almost), whatever you are doing, so you need to know – precisely – what you're supposed to be thinking of. That's why its (i.e. the JWT briefing document) full title is "the Summary of the Creative Brief".'

a) The trigger word

To borrow from the last *How to Plan Advertising* book, 'Words are like little bombs'. The right ones can explode inside us, demanding an original and exciting solution instead of a mediocre, pedestrian one. A creative's mind is like a 90mm Howitzer Field Gun. All the planner has to do is arm it and then point it in the right direction. Creative people will be perusing your brief – or listening at the briefing – for an exciting word or phrase that can trigger an idea. The sort of overall response you're looking for from your team is as follows: 'Ah. I never thought of it like that' (interestingly this is usually the first response one would like from a consumer).

Here are some more observations about 'Trigger words':

> 'A great brief makes our life difficult in the nicest possible way by giving us a damn good thought in the brief to which we have to apply lateral thinking to make it brilliant.'

> 'If the brief has an original angle, a creative should be embarrassed if the advertising doesn't.'

> 'It's when you can't stop thinking about it, and you go home with a key thought in your head from the briefing.'

> 'What you need is a one-line-portable-take-away thought.'

The planner should think carefully about every word on a brief; each one should be there for a reason – any word is potentially a spark plug which starts the engine.

l.

Some illustrative examples of 'trigger words':

1. Persil laundry detergent

Persil has a new Stain Release System. Persil releases 'clean' like no other laundry detergent.

This is the literal thought, but it is only a short mental leap to the lateral thought that is the commercial, which is centred around the metaphor of release or liberation. (See Storyboard 5.2.)

2. Black Magic chocolates

4.

Take Black Magic out of the kitchen and put it back into the bedroom.

This was written by the planner for a follow-up campaign after ingredients-based advertising featuring the different chocolates in the box.

b) The correct amount of facts

Deciding how much information to give the creative team is a fine art, and may vary by individual as well as by product category (another reason to know your team). There is a fine line between thoroughness and pedantic nonsense:

7.

2.

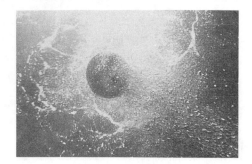

3.

5.

6.

8.

9.

Storyboard 5.2: Persil

10.

11.

12.

13.

14.

15.

Storyboard 5.2 (continued)

'Smart people give simple briefs.'

'Give me the freedom of a tightly defined strategy.'

'I've got a five-star engine. Don't give me two-star fuel.'

'The worst case scenario is an unattainable shopping list or wish list dressed up as thoroughness.'

'Simple and interesting are not mutually exclusive. Simple doesn't have to mean dull, pedestrian or basic. Gratuitous complexity doesn't help me.'

The consumer can only take away one thought so don't give the team charged with talking to the consumer eight things to say.

'I remember once a planner was always giving me briefs in which there were several points the client wanted us to get across about the brand. Tony, I said, you should know about the importance of the single-minded proposition, so never mind giving me one thought to describe this brand, try just giving me one word. 'Multi-faceted' came the reply.' (Don't do this!)

c) What do creatives actually DO with a brief?

It is important to remember that the purpose of most agencies' one-page creative brief format (as featured in the previous chapter) is to act as the summary of the creative briefing. It is usually used only as an *aide-memoire*. There are surprisingly large numbers of creatives who go straight to the middle box and read the key response (or proposition). And nothing else.

'Look for the prioritised fact.'

'Look for the phrase that will most likely link the desired response with the most appropriate stimulus.'

'I read the Single Most Important Thing section first. I'm about to take a journey. The other parts of the brief are the five stops on the way. But first of all, I want to know where I am going – it's a perfectly natural human thing to do.'

'I leave it on the desk and refer back to it. I never throw it away.'

'I look for something that I didn't know already so I can create something no one expected.'

4 What do creatives want from a briefing?

'A good briefing is when you can't wait for them to get out of the office so you can start.'

Everyone's heard the one about the laminated brief for Speedo swimwear and how it was thrown into a swimming pool for the creatives to retrieve. Or the one where the creatives were driven off in the boring family wagon for a briefing/test drive.

However, you can't always get the team offsite for every creative briefing meeting, given today's work load pressures and the fact that many briefs are for extensions of an existing successful campaign theme. The onus is therefore on you to make the briefing just as effective when it's held internally in the office as well as externally. Good ads are stories, bad ones are presentations, and it is exactly the same with briefings. And theatre is no substitute for relevance.

'I don't judge whether it was a good briefing or not as to whether I had fun.'

a) Make it relevant

It is massively important to get the context and descriptors right when you're briefing. Every creative person wants to write a famous campaign. The definition of a famous campaign is one that has permeated the national consciousness. One key aspect of this is 'relate-ability'. This is the means by which new themes get mixed up with perennial themes to make a compelling story that the target can relate to. This means spotting the recurring themes of our lives, stuff that comes up in the media repeatedly, identifying social trends that everyone can tap into. Current examples might be road rage, tele-working, travelling abroad, house husbands. Finger-on-the-pulse social observation is crucial to staying relevant, to being aware of what is going on in the world. Planners are very good at spotting social trends and these things can be a big help to creatives. One of the reasons the OXO family have lasted so long and remained fresh for decades is because the vehicle was able to encompass the advent of such things as vegetarianism among teenagers, microwaves and empty nesting. (See Storyboard 5.3.)

b) Make it clear

Most creatives are confident enough to be able to cope with 'the planner's ad' – which, however pedestrian, is usually a fair expression of how you see it in your mind's eye. This can be a really good exemplar of what the desired response is from the consumer. A brief for Kellogg's Cornflakes as the best cereal to wake up to was brought to life by the planner bearing two cereal bowls, one containing an alarm clock (representing Kellogg's Cornflakes), the other containing a pair of old slippers (representing two Weetabix biscuits). We got the drift.

1.

2.

3.

4.

5.

6.

Storyboard 5.3: Oxo

7.

8.

9.

'Keep it simple. I always ask first "What's the bottom line?" Then, "What are the details we need to discuss?"'

'Don't guide me down too many paths, just make sure I start from the right place'

'The best briefing I had lasted three minutes: "These people here, this is what they're like. This is what they don't know, and this is why it is important that they know it. This is the media, and you know those ads that so and so did for such and such brand? Well, we need to do that for this client."'

c) Make it interesting

Don't just hand the brief over and tell us to read it (or even worse, read it aloud). The bit of paper represents a pre-set agenda. Any self-respecting creative team will need to discuss it in the first instance rather than pre-accept it.

'I want to get the feeling that I am talking to the consumer.'

'Talk to me like a normal person. Don't pollute me with jargon when I'm about to speak to the consumer. "Yellow fats" is not a category *they* are familiar with.'

'We do a lot of talking and talking and not necessarily agreeing.'

'The planner should have the ability to inspire a desire to do things differently.'

d) Open doors rather than close them

One of the hardest things is judging between loose and tight. If the brief is too tight (such as too many executional guidelines or client-driven mandatories) then there is no room for the building blocks of inspiration, there is only room for a small squirt of glue to stick them all together. If the brief is too loose, then you'll end up with an amorphous mass that can't be shaped. It is important for the planner to help the client prioritise, to stop them pushing for an unattainable wish list. Clients will know their product better than anyone else does, but that does not necessarily mean they know their brand and how its benefits should be communicated better than their agency.

'I don't like to find myself being straitjacketed by a brief rather than be released by it.'

'You mustn't be too prescriptive. Give us some air.'

'Be a Visionary. Show me a place I hadn't thought of.'
(Simon Dicketts, M&C Saatchi)

'Good planners act as gardeners, not gatekeepers.'

The briefing rules for long-running campaigns (by which we mean those that have lasted for four years or more) are slightly different. Some long-running campaigns have always been penned by the same team (such as the Oxo family and the two Philadelphia secretaries). Those teams will have a pretty clear idea of how the campaign works and how the characters behave. A brand new team, however, will need a slightly different briefing on a long-running campaign. First off, you should give them a distillation of 'the story so far', and take them up to the end of the latest instalment. This will help them define where they can take the story from there. The secret is not to 'overbrief', for while the team need to get the founding elements correct, they also need to get an intuitive feel for where they can take the campaign. Half of a campaign's longevity is due to its ability to evolve, and keeping the plot fresh is key. Take, for example, 'Polo, the mint with the hole.' This campaign line has not changed in decades. The campaign idea is very much tonal – cheeky, irreverent, friendly, charming – so a Polo briefing has to be about encouraging an intuitive feeling for what is right.

5 Follow-up time – what's needed?

What happens when the creative idea is born – what is the planner's contribution to creativity now?

- *The internal presentation*, i.e. when the creatives first present their finished idea to the account team/management (there will usually have been informal discussions prior to this as the idea was evolving/emerging, when there were questions they wanted answers to).

  The creative team have created a vehicle on which to carry the proposition. It should be true to the brief, relevant to the target audience and creatively distinctive. They are the best ones to give a truly comprehensive exposition of their vision.

- *The client presentation*

  In most UK agencies the account people present the work (although this is changing as our work practices become Americanised). Planners should then step up to the plate and be great translators of the anticipated consumer response for the client's benefit. If the client trusts the planner's judgement and insight, the planner becomes a priceless commodity for the creative team.

- *The communications pre-test research debrief*

  Many clients invest in animatic and concept testing prior to production. Many still use it as a 'traffic light' (go/stop) rather than a diagnostic tool to better understand how an idea is working against its target audience.

  In the case of explaining the results, good, bad or curate's egg, to the creative team, the same rules apply as for the briefing. Just tell us what's happened in the consumer's mind and why.

- *The role for planning in the pre-production/production process*

  Keep your noses out of pre-production is our view! And you are welcome to the shoot as long as you don't do anything more than eat a bacon sandwich!

6 What do creatives dislike about planners?

'Fact Nazis'

Facts alone are not enough – it's what they mean that makes them significant.

'Rigid thinkers'

Dogmatic, blinker-wearing planners who can only see in straight lines are not going to help creatives see around corners. Debate, flexibility, insight and intuition are all good tools to better relationships.

'Those that lack passion for advertising'

Many planners come from a research background – but we won't let that put us off!

'The planner who wants to be the Creative Director'
'They need to be satisfied with their role as a planner'

Again, there is the fine line between the planner describing his own workmanlike vision for the ad and then thinking it actually is an ad.

'Messengers for the research'

Data dump debriefs are meaningless to innumerate creatives; it is not enough to tell us what happened – we need to know why.

'Lazy thinking. They haven't tried hard enough'

Self-evident. The brief with the proposition 'best tasting' isn't going to help anyone develop good advertising.

'Turning simplistic thinking into pseudo rocket science is the worst crime against creativity'

Most creatives are simple folk. They also have quite well-developed bullshit detectors.

'In the valley of the bland, the one idea man is king!'
It is all about stimulation and challenge.

A planner should be the sort of person you'd want to have a conversation with anyway, only this particular conversation is to result in some advertising.

7 Ten tips for top planners

(or how to make everything you touch seem better for it)

Can you answer the following questions about the creative team you are currently working with?

1. What are their proudest achievements? What do they consider to be their best work? What are their goals going forward?
2. How do they like to be briefed? Do they like propositions or responses? What briefs or briefings have they found helpful or unhelpful in the past?
3. Are they knowledge junkies or fact freaks or proponents of the one-word brief?
4. Do they like to be involved in all the preliminary strategic discussions, review the brief, even write their own propositions or prefer to wait for a clean direction?
5. When and how often do they want to see you again after the briefing – daily visits bearing additional information or head round the door to ask if they need anything? Are you dealing with Greta Garbo or Baby Jane?

And five things that you should do for yourself:

1. Read anything by Bill Bernbach.
2. Think positive. Don't come back to the creatives after the client meeting or the research debrief with a problem unless you've got half a solution.
3. Deliver a client the agency can do business with.
4. Be on their side. One creative once described the planner as a parrot that sits on your shoulder and whispers gently in your ear – whilst simultaneously crapping down your back!
5. Listen hard.

6 Creative development research

Jackie Boulter

Introduction

The business problem has been identified. The role that advertising can play in solving that problem has been isolated. The advertising strategy to do it has been explored, and the creative brief has been written. The client says – 'I think we should research the idea before we can give go-ahead to production'. What do we do? Creative development research.

In this chapter we will discuss any market research conducted between the stage of agreeing an advertising strategy and the appearance of finished advertising in the chosen media. Conventionally, creative development research refers to market research carried out on advertising *ideas*, prior to production, but in recent years it has encompassed early exploratory research as well. In this chapter we will cover all stages of such research. This definition, however, will be further refined into creative development research and creative pre-testing. We will define creative development research as research (usually qualitative) on an advertising idea prior to production, and pre-testing as quantitative research on finished production (or occasionally animatics or concepts) prior to appearance in the media.

It's important to understand the context in which the research is judged, as manifested by the difference in terminology. The term *pre-testing* implies a pass/fail judgement of a creative idea; the term creative *development* implies the idea is still 'work in progress' to be developed to its optimum.

Why do research at this stage?

As stated in the introduction to this chapter, creative development research is research conducted at the initial stage when creative ideas have been agreed, but *before* a finished advertisement is produced. The reason for doing the research is fairly straightforward: to answer the question . . . *Is the advertising likely to meet the objectives set for it?* The first rule of creative development research, therefore, is to ensure that you and the client are in agreement as to the role of and strategy for advertising. By this I mean getting answers to the fundamental questions that formed the basis of the advertising strategy, i.e: What do we expect the *advertising* to do, as opposed to any other element of the marketing mix?

- *Who* are we advertising to?
- *What* do we want them to feel as a result of seeing the advertising?
- *How*, specifically, can advertising be used to do it – *what* should it say?

It is only when you are sure that all parties have agreed that these objectives are what needs to be investigated, that a brief for research should be written.

To establish whether the advertising is likely to meet its objectives, the research must be able to distinguish between three different elements of the advertising, and report on each separately. These three elements are: the advertising *strategy*, the advertising *idea* and the advertising *execution*.

The advertising strategy

Two chapters have already been written in this book about the advertising strategy: 'The role for advertising', and 'Developing advertising strategy'. Both chapters emphasised the need to isolate the optimum usage of advertising in helping to solve a business problem, the role that advertising, and no other element of the marketing mix, can do to aid a client's business. Once a creative team have come up with a creative idea, the role of creative development research is to explore whether or not the strategy worked when it was translated into a consumer message . . . were we right when we said that by speaking to a certain set of people in a certain way, and telling them a certain message, we would get them to *feel* a certain way which would benefit our brand in the way we'd hoped? In other words, was the advertising strategy correct? And, most importantly, did we manage to *communicate* it to our consumer?

The advertising idea

The art of advertising is to communicate the strategy to consumers in a way which will have impact, and to create a relationship between the consumer and the brand. Advertising recognises that a relationship can be built by either communicating *rational* bits of information, or by creating an *emotional* response, or by a combination of both. Good strategic research will have established which communication route will get the response we want (the 'how' and the 'what to say' questions of advertising strategy). The job of the creative team is to take the direction given in the creative brief to come up with a *creative idea* which becomes the *form* to the strategy's *content*. The role of creative development research is to ensure that if the *message* of the strategy is sound, the *messenger* (i.e., the idea) manages to communicate it in the best way possible. And if not, why not?

The execution

The advertising idea is usually the element in the advertising that consumers recognise as a campaign: the bit that a consumer will use to describe an ad to someone else – for example, the BT ads using Bob Hoskins, the Andrex Puppy ads, 'the world drinks Coke' ads, and so on. Each campaign, however, consists of a number of different *executions:* a number of ads which make up a whole. Each execution itself has a slightly different message, or a slightly different way of saying the same message, and, of course, consists of different *executional elements* which could affect how the consumer receives the message from the messenger. Consumers might agree with the strategy, and respond in principle to the idea, but dislike how it is done – e.g. is a spokesperson a good idea, but the one we chose irritates? Would a woman be better than a man as hero in the ad? Does a conversation in the ad send signals we hadn't intended? Is a poster a good idea and the line used correct, but the type illegible? And so on. These responses are all important, because they *can* get in the way of the advertising working properly. They can be changed so that you're more likely to listen to what the advertising has to say. However, if you don't separate these responses from responses to the message itself, you run the risk of either rejecting work which could work, or in accepting work where people like the execution but ignore the message about brand, in which case the work will be ineffective and wasted.

So when the research is being undertaken, it's important that answers be given to a number of questions:

- Is the strategy sound – will our message meet with the right intended response? (If no, we go back to doing further strategic development.)
- If yes, have we communicated it in a way which will be *impactful* and *appropriate for the brand?*
- If not, is it because the advertising *idea* is wrong, or is it because the *execution* of the idea is hindering, not helping?
- Can we make it better? Did we learn anything which will improve it further?

The qualitative vs quantitative debate

Over the years there has been a considerable amount of debate regarding the benefits and drawbacks of qualitative vs quantitative research at this stage of advertising development. In line with many authors, I believe that the best approach is to recognise that there are horses for courses. Qualitative and quantitative research are *both* valid research techniques, and are both used extensively in the development of advertising. The debate should not be an either/or one, but rather one about the criteria for deciding the *appropriateness* of one or the other, or indeed, *within* any broad methodology, which type of qualitative or quantitative research is best in any particular instance.

a) Qualitative research

Why is qualitative research so useful in helping to develop advertising? The reasons are to do with the nature of qualitative research. It is exploratory, non-directive and sensitive. It allows the moderator or interviewer to discover *why* people hold the opinions they do, in a relaxed, non-threatening environment. Group discussions allow the free flow of ideas which encourages individuals to investigate their attitudes more deeply and thoughtfully than other kinds of research will allow. Depth interviews allow an interviewer to create the kind of environment in which sensitive subjects can be explored. In this way, qualitative research is a more *flexible* methodology, helping us to understand how and why people respond to the advertising idea in the way that they do.

However, there are drawbacks. Qualitative research can not tell you conclusively whether or not a piece of advertising will break through the advertising clutter: whether it communicates as much when seen in the context of a night's viewing as it does on its own in a research environment: whether it will 'perform' as well as other executions or other campaigns at other times. The relative importance of answering these questions will help you determine whether qualitative creative development (at all, or on its own) is appropriate or not.

b) Quantitative research

Quantitative research, when conducted properly, allows you to measure response to an advertisement on a number of pre-defined criteria: impact, communication, comprehension, claimed likelihood of trial, and so on. As a quantitative questionnaire is administered individually, and there is no room for interviewer interpretation, theoretically any statistically significant differences are real ones. This allows differences between sub-sets of respondents, or different campaigns or different executions within a campaign to be accurately measured, and for norms to be established.

However, there are inevitable limitations:

- Respondents can only answer those questions that are asked. If there's an issue with the advertising that hasn't been anticipated, the information may be lost.
- The natural reticence of the British public may mean that their true feelings are not admitted to; would you admit to an interviewer that an ad made you feel sexy, envious, insecure? If not, possibly others feel the same way.
- As the questionnaire must be administered as designed, there is little opportunity to use responses in a way to think how the ad could be altered or improved – little chance to say 'If you feel X, *what if* they did Y?'

Having discussed some of the big issues and theories surrounding this topic, let's turn now to the mechanics of how it's done.

CREATIVE DEVELOPMENT RESEARCH

Classical creative development research as we've defined it, is qualitative in nature, in order to allow the moderator to explore how and why the advertising idea is working or not, and therefore to aid in developing the creative work fully. In general, there are two broad stages of research, which we'll call:

* Initial exploratory research.
* Standard creative development research.

▌nitial exploratory research

Once a brief has been given to a creative team, they may wish to explore the options thrown up by the brief before settling for a creative recommendation. In this way they can gain more understanding about how consumers might respond to a broad creative *approach*.

A case history – Cow & Gate

Cow & Gate was a brand that had been supported over a number of years by promoting its sub-brands. The decision was taken to support the core Cow & Gate brand in order to increase saliency and trial. (Early trial is essential as baby food is relevant only for the first 12 months of the child's life.)

A strategy was produced to strengthen the core brand, but there was a real need to define the differential on which the brand campaign would rest. The agency decided to conduct a large qualitative project on brand identity – its scope and unique attributes.

The research was carried out as group discussions amongst first-time mums of babies under six months and pregnant mums. Whilst the most commonly used projective techniques such as personalising the company and managing director helped redefine the problem (e.g. old-fashioned and recessive) three exercises yielded positive creative direction.

* *A discussion of modern parenthood* defined motherhood as being about enjoying the time you had with your baby rather than being the baby's drudge. This finding liberated the creative team, allowing them to change the mental setting of the advertising from the industry stereotype of the highchair in the kitchen to the world outside. They now understood the 'mums' they were talking to.
* *Visual images depicting the brand (Visual 6.1)* In each group mothers were given an identical set of magazines and asked to tear out anything, 'however silly' that reminded them of the brand. Consistently across the group they chose tender and intimate pictures of mothers with small babies and pictures of the English

countryside, which they did for no other brand. Cow & Gate's 'image board', therefore, was very different from those for the competition (Visual 6.2).

- *Recognition of the logo (Visual 6.3)* We asked consumers to draw both the Heinz and Cow & Gate logos from memory, which not only helped us gauge how memorable they were, but to see what were the strongest components. One of the most dominant features for Cow & Gate was the large red ampersand ('&').

Visual 6.1:
Cow & Gate image

Visual 6.2:
SMA image

Visual 6.3:
Cow & Gate logo board

The creative idea work sprang organically from this project, with both press and television advertising, firstly in press, with its spontaneous outdoor 'snapshots' of parents and babies in a summer landscape (Visual 6.4), and then followed with television (Storyboard 6.1). It would not have emerged without the learning from this piece of developmental research.

Standard creative development research

The point of this stage of research is to gain early consumer feedback to the advertising idea at a stage before substantial money has been committed to production. In order to do this, the idea has to be presented to potential consumers in a way that is understandable and sums up the thinking so far. The tangible way the idea is presented is the 'stimulus material', and this can come in a number of forms:

Stimulus material

1. Television/Cinema

- *Narrative tapes:* An audio tape where a voice-over artist describes the television ad, and narrates any dialogue from the ad. It attempts to give a flavour of the advertising tone.

1.

Visual 6.4:
Cow & Gate press advertising

2.

- *Tapes and boards:* Often a narrative tape is accompanied by a few selected key visuals – usually a few drawings to explain the action or general 'look' of the ad.
- *Storyboards and soundtrack:* This is a tape consisting only of the soundtrack, including any music or sound effects, accompanied by a number of drawings on boards to visualise the 'action'. The moderator would expose the boards in the correct sequence and time as dictated by the soundtrack.
- *Animatics:* Key frames from the commercial are drawn, and filmed on video alongside the soundtrack. Often movement can be incorporated into the drawings in a 'cartoon' fashion.
- *Photomatics/Stealomatics:* Actual photographs or film clips are used, and edited to produce the storyline of the commercial, along with a soundtrack, and filmed on video.

1.

2.

3.

4.

5.

6.

Storyboard 6.1:
Cow & Gate television advertising

2. Print

To investigate initial responses to either press or poster advertising, we usually need to research 'rough' concepts, i.e, drawings of the ad, or a simply-set mocked-up ad. These concepts can be either highly finished with headline, copy, pack shot photograph, etc., or a simple line drawing of the ad with no copy attached.

3. Radio

As it is singularly cheap to produce a radio ad, it is often the case that a decision is made to make it, then research the finished ad. If it works, fine; if it doesn't it's back to the drawing board to produce another one. Rarely is there a need for an interim piece of stimulus material.

One of the key roles of a planner is to determine which type of stimulus material would be most appropriate at this stage of research. As the research is being conducted in order to determine whether or not the idea is sound, it's critical that the respondents in the research see the *idea* in a way which is understandable and uses the right tone of voice. Each type of stimulus material has benefits and drawbacks:

- *Television* – is movement important to communicate the idea? Is the visual style langorous or fast – is that important? Does the idea depend upon the visuals, for example, a visual gag? Most importantly, can the idea be translated into an animatic style or is it wholly dependent upon production values? If so, is a description which allows consumers' imagination to run riot, or a good stealomatic a better option than a simple animatic?
- *Print* – press can be difficult to research as the ad's success is almost wholly dependent upon finished production values. Certainly communication, comprehension and strategic intent can be assessed, and the question to ask is how finished the concept needs to be for the idea to be understood.

Ask yourself these questions when advertising routes are due to go into creative development research. Talk to the creative team to make sure you understand the advertising idea, and then between you try to decide what form of stimulus material would most easily represent the idea to respondents in research. Try not to allow practical issues such as timing ('We need to do the research this week so we won't have time to make an animatic') or political or client pressure ('We always do animatics, it's what the Chief Executive understands') influence your decision. It's one of the most critical stages in the advertising development process, and one where the answers you get can depend almost entirely on the material you use.

Choice of research moderator

The other key role a planner has is in determining which company or moderator is appropriate for conducting the research. In some agencies, including my own, it is often the case that the planner carries out this research him/herself. In other agencies, and for some clients, this function is done by an independent qualitative market researcher. Apart from the philosophical reasons for the research being done by an 'insider' or an 'outsider', the requirements of the research remain the same; your choice of who to use to do it will depend on their understanding of the importance of certain fundamentals:

(a) Research methodology

Given the premise that creative development research is exploratory in nature, qualitative research is the norm. Qualitative research takes a number of forms, and again, it's important to decide on your objectives for the research before making a decision as to the kind of method you will use.

The key types are:

- *Group discussions* (or 'focus groups' in America). Groups are the most often-used form of qualitative research when developing television advertising; other sub-sets of them, such as mini-groups, friendship groups, etc., are used for certain target audiences. A group discussion traditionally consists of seven or eight respondents, recruited to fulfil certain demographic/brand usership criteria, then invited to the recruiter's home or a specialist central viewing facility, for a discussion with a group moderator who skilfully conducts it in order to uncover their responses to the advertising. Having a number of respondents helps the free flow and cross-fertilisation of ideas, debate and explanation of viewpoints in a way that helps the moderator *understand* how and why the advertising works (or not).

  However, one has to be conscious of the natural tendency of individuals in a group to want to build rapport with each other, which may interfere with uncovering *individual* responses. Good moderators will use techniques to ensure they capture any initial responses or viewpoints (such as asking them to write down their spontaneous views before starting the discussion), separately from the group's more studied discussion wherever appropriate.

- *Mini-groups/Friendship groups:* These follow the same principles and procedure of standard group discussions, the major difference being the number and type of people in the group. Mini-groups typically have four or five respondents, and are used as a halfway point between a group (where the *contrast* of views is helpful) and a depth interview (where an *individual's* view is the optimum). They are often used for creative development of print advertising, or for more complicated or specialist top-ics – business groups, finance, and so on.

Friendship groups are those where one deliberately recruits friends to the group as we know the respondents will feel more comfortable, relaxed and therefore willing to express their true views. Children and teenagers are often researched in this way.

- *Depth interviews.* Individual depth interviews are, as their name implies, one-to-one interviewing between a skilled moderator and a respondent. Depths are often used in cases where the target audience is either so diverse that their individual experiences are too different for a group viewpoint to be formulated, or where the subject matter is so sensitive that true and honest responses would not emerge in the more public group forum.

Depth interviews are often used to develop press advertising on the premise that this most closely replicates the environment in which a press (or print) ad is experienced. While this is true, the question one must ask is whether or not you will be able to uncover how an individual would really respond in such a situation, or whether the slightly more artificial mini-group approach would give you more understanding. This is because:

- depths can be more frightening to the respondent – they may feel more on the spot than they would in a group.
- the lack of a format encouraging the free flow of ideas may lead to a more *rational* response.

These concerns must be balanced against the legitimate concern that a group response might suppress some important individual viewpoints. Again, work out what's important for *this* piece of research and make a recommendation based on that.

(b) Sampling

It's easy to say but often forgotten that advertising rarely is intended to work against all people. Most advertising has a defined target audience which is a sub-set of the total pop-ulation. The advertising strategy aims to affect *those people only* in a certain way. Clearly when conducting advertising research it's important that the research be carried out amongst those people. Don't allow yourself to be distracted by requests to interview other audiences (e.g. 'Last time we spoke to mothers as well as children') unless there is a legit-imate reason for doing so. Creative development research is about assessing an idea against a specific advertising strategy; keep the sample tight and single-minded to reflect the strategic intent.

(c) Analysis and interpretation

Qualitative research is about interpretation, not reportage. When you decide to carry out research to develop advertising, you need a moderator who understands how advertising works as outlined earlier. As qualitative research is not a laboratory test, but depends on interpretation of the things people say coupled with non-verbal responses, it is vital that you choose an advertising-sensitive moderator to do the research. Not all qualitative researchers are the same; some highly respected members of the profession would agree that their expertise lies elsewhere.

The key requirement is for someone who understands how to present the findings in a way which provides actionable, diagnostic guidelines. The research is not an end in itself; it's a guide to development for a creative team. The research must be able to answer the question – 'So what do we need to do?' It is the planner's responsibility to provide clear, actionable feedback to the creative team.

BT Advertising: a case history

AMV had been asked to pitch for the BT Personal Communications account. The brief from the Client was clearly to get people to make more and longer calls, and one way of doing this was to get men in particular to do this. The agency developed a two-pronged strategy which would 1) tackle men head on, by raising the status of female-style 'small talk' in men's eyes to encourage men to reappraise their own behaviour, and 2) legitimise women's behaviour . . . both in their own eyes and in the eyes of their men, often the gatekeepers of the phone and the bill. In addition to this, the creative vehicle needed to be able to give more 'hard sell' messages such as announcements of price reductions and new services.

The creative team came up with the idea of a presenter, who could communicate that 'It's good to talk' in a way which would be equally appealing to men and women. Bob Hoskins was used in the initial scripts which were tested as photomatics (Storyboard 6.2), but other potential presenters were investigated. Bob was found to work as he was a 'hard man' whom men would respect (even if he gave a 'soft' message), but women find endearing.

In the creative development stage the planner investigated a number of scripts using Bob in different ways. Two key pointers emerged:

- Bob worked best as a consumer ombudsman, rather than a BT presenter, when he's seen to be working for the customer, not the company. As one respondent said: *'He's my informer.'*
- The 'ghost' technique was crucial; Bob needed to dip in and out of the action without being noticed by others, rather than *presenting* in the more traditional way. *'Used like that he's more telling than selling.'*

The other strand of the strategy was to communicate the *value* of a phone call. It became clear in the research that comparing the cost of a call to other everyday purchases, would help people reassess their attitude to phone usage. This learning was directly translated into poster concepts. (Visual 6.5.)

1. Bob: 'It's all right, he can't see me.'

2. Alex: 'I'm just calling before we pop out to the cinema – see how you are . . .'

3. Wife: ' . . . I know what I meant to ask, that dress you were looking for . . . did you find one with the neck you wanted – square wasn't it, not too low . . .'

4. Alex's mother (laughing): 'Don't be daft, I'm past that . . . it's for whist, not whistles . . .'

5. Bob: 'Call at the weekend. Low weekend rates means a 20-minute chat costs less than a bottle of lager.'

6. Alex: 'I hear you're buying low-cut dresses . . .'

Storyboard 6.2: BT Photomatic

Visual 6.5: BT poster concepts

CREATIVE PRE-TESTING

We will define 'pre-testing' (or 'copy testing' in America) as any research carried out on *finished* creative work (that is, after production) but prior to the advertising appearing on air or in print. (Some companies claim this research can be done on unfinished creative work, for example animatics; in all other respects the thinking remains the same.) The reason for conducting this type of research is to aid client's and agency's judgement as to whether a piece of advertising is good or not, and as such is more evaluative than developmental. In many cases client and/or agency feel uncomfortable about making such a judgement until the finished ad is exposed in its final recommended form to consumers, and their responses can be gauged. In many cases there is a belief that this must be done *quantitatively* – e.g. when advertising will appear in more than one market – or where there is an underlying concern about qualitative research's remit for interpretation.

If the decision has been made to carry out quantitative pre-testing, the planner should always ensure that the *methodology* be appropriate for the advertising objectives *in this case*. There are many forms of quantitative pre-testing, and not all will be appropriate at all times. Some research companies will tell you otherwise; they have a belief that all advertising works in a particular way, and have consequently developed a technique to measure the advertising's ability to do so. Some clients also prefer 'testing' ads with a familiar methodology, time after time, irrespective of the different objectives for different campaigns. Don't allow yourself to be seduced into conducting research in this way just because it's the way it's always done; each piece of advertising is unique, and should be treated as such.

A planner should, therefore, attempt to get all parties to focus on the real questions:

- How do we think advertising works?
- What do we expect this particular ad to do in this case?
- Which type of research method will give us the most appropriate guidance?

Once agreement is reached on these fundamental issues, you can start to assess research methodologies and decide which one is the best for you.

The choice of methodology

The difference between quantitative methodologies usually rests upon different beliefs in the way advertising works. It is my contention that not all ads work in the same way. Some research companies agree, and have developed approaches to testing which build in recognition of this, and offer a more flexible assessment procedure; others believe there is only one way that advertising works, and their technique will evaluate in that way only. *If* your advertising objective and strategy matches this belief, then their approach is a valid one; if not it isn't. In other words, any of the approaches discussed in this chapter are valid, *as long as they are evaluating your ad on the correct criteria.* As we've been saying throughout this chapter, research is only an aid to judgement, not an end in itself; any research is only useful if it helps you to judge whether the advertising meets the objectives. Work out your objectives and strategy, and use research to develop and evaluate advertising against them only.

The quantitative pre-testing marketplace can be divided broadly into two groups: *persuasion or attitude shift* techniques, and *impact and communication* techniques.

Persuasion tests are based upon a simple model of advertising, a belief that exposure to an advertising message should directly convert into sales, and that this can be predictive of marketplace behaviour. This can be done either by comparing the views of a sample pre- and post-exposure, or by contrasting a test and control sample, or as a variation, by comparing responses to those seeing the ad on television vs those who haven't (Day after Recall).

Typically, these studies work by recruiting a sample to a location ostensibly to view a television programme within which ads are inserted. They are asked to choose their preferred brands from a list of product areas prior to viewing, and again after viewing. Comparisons between the two sets of data are compared, and an uplift in propensity to buy is seen as an indication of advertising effectiveness.

Most persuasion testing has been done on fmcg brands, and, arguably, is more appropriate for 'new news' than for brand reinforcement messages when maintaining brand loyalty and behaviour is the objective rather than conquest purchasing.

Impact and communication tests measure intermediate constructs such as impact, brand recall, likes/dislikes, 'diagnostics' (i.e, attitudes towards the advertising). Usually this is done by showing a reel of ads to a target audience sample in which the test ad is imbedded. While it arguably allows a more flexible approach to pre-testing than persuasion tests, it does raise the questions as to what is deemed to be a good result, and which, if any, of the measures will be predictive. This approach demands clear interpretation of the results for client and agency understanding, and requires more judgement on their behalf.

Key measures

A number of 'hybrid' methodologies have also been produced over the years which use elements of both these approaches. Whatever the methodology, however, there are certain key measures that are commonly assessed; the planner's task is to select which are appropriate given the way in which the advertising is intended to work.

Impact/Standout

At its most direct level, an ad must gain the attention of the target audience. Testing methodology will try to assess:

* Has the advertising captured the audience's attention?
* Is it memorable over time?
* Is its memorability good or poor relative to other ads?

Brand recall

A measure of how well the brand name registered.

Communication

This is usually defined as the ability of an advertisement to deliver the desired message in an understandable and believable way. It is usually a good idea to leave this section of the questionnaire as open-ended as possible, in order to allow the respondent to inter-pret the ad in his or her own way.

Brand image measurement

In many cases an ad is not trying to get the viewer to take a particular action, (e.g. 'Buy now while stocks last') but to *feel* a particular way about a brand. It is sometimes impor-tant to assess how advertising works to achieve a change or reinforcement of brand image.

Involvement

Involvement is best defined as the *quality of impact*. An ad which involves the viewer is one which is read or watched more carefully, and therefore better remembered, which communicates more powerfully and therefore probably recalled for longer.

Persuasion

Persuasion, or intent to purchase, is linked to the issue of respondents' change in atti-tude to the brand on exposure to the advertising. This measure is predicated on the belief that advertising works by *persuading* the viewer to buy the product advertised, and that this change can take place after one or two viewings in a test situation. It is often a single measure which is evaluated against a bank of 'normative data' – that is, the abil-ity to persuade – and is often used by some companies as the only necessary measure to assess an ad's likely effectiveness.

Likeability

A more recent measure of an ad's likely effectiveness has been its likeability. Famously, the American Research Foundation ran a Copy Validity Project to test the effectiveness of different pre-testing research methodologies to settle the debate once and for all as to which method was most likely to accurately predict a sales effect. The one measure which did best was likeability. Whereas the results were not true in 100 per cent of cases, it seems to be common sense that ads which are better liked will be better remembered and understood, and therefore more effective.

Diagnostics

To evaluate the advertising on the above criteria will tell you whether or not you met the objectives as hoped; what they won't do is explain *why* it did, or *why not* if it didn't. Diag-nostic information is, in essence, quantification of the kind of understanding you gain from qualitative creative development research, and is invaluable in helping you to understand the results you've achieved on key measures. It will also give guidance as to why it is deficient if it is, so that you can do something about it either now or in future advertising.

Some points to consider

Whichever research methodology you choose, however, there are three key issues to bear in mind:

1. The use of normative data

Many research companies sell their techniques on the basis of normative results; they believe that a comparison across time of all tests will provide a framework for success against which any test ad can be measured. This is often a highly seductive promise for clients who prefer the certainty of results, but can be illusory. As we've said before, an ad that 'works well' may have different success levels for different target audiences or in different markets; financial advertising will perform differently from confectionery, for example. If broad comparisons are going to be made, make sure you're comparing like with like.

2. Holistic vs atomistic evaluation

Some research techniques attempt to break down a piece of communication into small sections (which can be as little as two or three seconds) and report on each section in turn: for example, by asking respondents to manipulate a 'joystick' or press buttons to register those parts of the ad that they like better or less. I would argue that it's better to assess an ad as a whole piece of communication rather than a collection of individual seconds. Certainly you'd want to know if there's an element in an ad which causes confusion, but don't be seduced by researchers who say that, e.g. the first three seconds are boring, can you fix it – that's rather like saying 'Hamlet' would be a better play if you took out the boring bits . . .

3. Interpretation

Ultimately, *any* findings from research, either qualitative or quantitative, will be interpreted by the researcher involved. By briefing him or her thoroughly, and by remaining involved throughout the process, you can help to ensure that the interpretation is sound: that the correct 'weighting' is applied to the different findings within the research, based upon your advertising objectives. All research must be viewed in the right context.

In conclusion

The key thought that this chapter should leave with you is that advertising works in a number of ways. At any stage of researching advertising ideas it is important to isolate how you think advertising will work in *this* instance, against *this* audience. This viewpoint can only be arrived at by *understanding* the consumers and what makes them tick.

Having this understanding will help you to prioritise their responses to the advertising, and aid in interpreting their views.

The question, therefore, is not a simple one of qualitative vs quantitative research or one technique vs another, but *which* kind of research will help you to understand if the advertising is working in the way intended. Almost any research technique currently on the market will help you to do this in some way; but always ensure that each technique is judged *each* time as to whether it will give you the information you need.

The role of the planner throughout the process is to keep sight of the advertising objectives, to ensure that research does not become an aim in itself, but is properly used as an aid to judgement. At every stage, from briefing a researcher to interpreting the findings for a creative team, keep in control; don't lose sight of what you're intending to do. Ultimately, the advertising will be successful if it has moved the audience in a particular way; remember that *this* is the true measure of advertising effectiveness.

7 Campaign evaluation

Paul Feldwick

The time has come when advertising has in some hands reached the status of a science. It is based on fixed principles and is reasonably exact. The causes and effects have been analysed until they are well understood. The correct methods of procedure have been proved and established. We know what is most effective, and we act on basic laws. Advertising, once a gamble, has thus become, under able direction, one of the safest of business ventures.

Claude Hopkins, *Scientific Advertising* (1922)

The effect of most advertising, it should be noted, is as difficult to quantify as, say, the efficacy of prayer . . . Most advertising efforts go out like acts of faith and hope into silent darkness, producing so little in the way of specific identifiable results that a whole industry has sprung up to provide audience measuring services, and reassurance, and thereby sustain the flagging will.

Frank Rowsome, *Think Small,* The Story of Volkswagen Advertising (1970)

Introduction

Advertising is an expensive business. Those who spend money on it should want to know what results they're getting. And those who plan and create it should want to find out if what they're doing is working; and how, and why it's working (or not), in order to learn how to do it better next time.

So everyone would like it if the process of evaluating advertising results were simple, precise, and reliable. Unfortunately, it is nearly always none of these.

Because of this, people often jump one of two ways. Some are tempted to believe too much; they take results at their face value, which may be misleading, or credit data with a degree of accuracy and reliability that isn't justified. Others become complete sceptics, which is a handy excuse for not bothering with evaluation at all.

Both errors have been around for a very long time, and have co-existed quite happily. The literature of advertising is full of quotes stressing the difficulty, or impossibility, of measuring advertising effects, especially on sales. These are counterpointed by a long succession of claims from researchers, ad agencies, and others, that they have at last found 'the answer' to the problem. Such contradictory signals lead to an understandable feeling of uneasiness among advertisers and their agencies – that an ideal answer exists somewhere, or is perhaps just about to exist, but no one is quite sure what or where it is.

And so, despite the general view that campaign evaluation ought to be a 'good thing', too often little or nothing is actually being done about it. I write this from experience: despite all the breast-beating and all the conferences on the subject, I am still surprised by how low a priority advertising evaluation often seems to be – both for advertisers and for account planners. This is especially true in most markets outside the UK; it is, perhaps surprisingly, largely true in the USA.

Let us start then by saying to all those who feel like this: don't worry about the fact that you have not yet found the Holy Grail. You're not the only ones. In fact, you're right to be confused. There is, for most situations, no solution that is simple, precise and reliable. There is likewise no single solution that is equally suitable for all cases. Evaluating the effects of advertising will involve you in thinking, judgement – and almost certainly, will cost money.

That's the bad news. The good news is, there is a wide range of possibilities available – and used intelligently, and often in conjunction with each other, it should be possible to get useful feedback on what is happening as a result of your advertising, and why. The numerous researchers and others who have developed different approaches to advertising evaluation over the last 75 years have each (in most cases anyway) left us with a technique that is useful for something. We just have to be a bit wary of frequent overclaims that suggest any of them had a universal or infallible answer. Claude Hopkins, quoted at the head of this chapter, was more right than wrong in the context of mail order advertising, where he had all his experience. His mistake was believing that the same principles would apply to all advertising.

Used thoughtfully, the available techniques for evaluating advertising should always be able to improve the quality and efficiency of your advertising over time. They will increase the chances of killing useless campaigns before it's too late, and just as important, provide evidence to persist with campaigns that do work. This is not to say that they will answer all problems, or necessarily 'optimise' anything. But studying how consumers actually respond to advertising in the marketplace is one of the key areas where the account planner can acquire relevant information and understanding.

And in order to measure effectiveness, we need to think hard about what sort of effects we expect. What exactly will consumers do if they respond to the campaign? What will go on in their minds? What will they need to take from our communications? We need to be very precise about the answers to such questions, and this in itself is a valuable discipline.

Sales effects versus consumer effects

There are two basic ways we could define advertising 'effects'. We can look at what happens to *sales* (orders, money changing hands, boxes moving out of shops). Or we can look at what happens to *people* who are exposed to the ads: what do they remember, how do their awareness or perceptions or behaviour change.

Each of these might be interesting, for different reasons.

Sales, or its equivalent in a non-commercial context, is always the ultimate goal of advertising. It's true that sales may sometimes only be influenced by advertising over the long term, or in conjunction with other activities (which are reasons why we might want to measure other things to isolate an advertising effect in the short term); but in the end the purpose of advertising is to benefit business. In other words, we want to sell more, or more profitably, with advertising than we would without it.

Consumer responses, on the other hand, can tell us much that sales alone generally can't, about *how* the advertising is (or isn't) working. *Who* is being influenced by the advertising? What are they noticing or remembering about it? How are their perceptions of the brand changing?

But consumer responses have also often been used to supplement, or even substitute for, sales results, as the ultimate measure of advertising 'success'. Sometimes this is inevitable – because in some categories it is very difficult to get reliable data on consumer sales, or market share. But it is important to remember that consumer responses are all in varying degrees remote from, and not a reliable proxy for, actual sales information. Increases in advertising awareness, or brand awareness, or positive brand attitudes, may all be useful learning, either for diagnostic reasons or if we believe they are 'leading indicators' of a sales response that may take longer to appear. But none of these is the same as a sales response.

Type of advertising effect	Relevant research
Exposure to advertising	Media research
Recall of advertising	Survey research
Attitudes to/communication of advertising	Survey/qualitative research
Awareness of brand	Survey research
Perceptions/image of brand	Survey/qualitative research
Attitude to brand	Survey/qualitative research
Claimed consumer behaviour	Survey research
Consumer buying behaviour	Panel data
Sales	Retail audit, consumer audit, ex-factory data

Figure 7.1: The commonest measures of 'advertising effect,
organised in order of their remoteness from sales

For many years, influential writers on advertising argued that sales were, for practical purposes, an irrelevant measure of advertising effect. Rosser Reeves (1961) wrote:

> Recently a group of marketing men, almost idly, at a luncheon table, listed 37 different factors, any or all of which could cause the total sales of a brand to move up or down.
>
> Advertising was only one of these.
>
> The product may be wrong. Price may be at fault. Distribution may be poor. The sales force may not be adequate. Budget may be too low. A better product may be sweeping the market. A competitor may be outwitting you with strong deals. There are many variables.
>
> And when a wheel has many spokes, who can say which spoke is supporting the wheel?

Sales responses to advertising can be hard to detect, so there is some truth in this. But for many years this had the unfortunate consequence of putting sales results off the evaluation agenda altogether. As a result, it has often been forgotten that all 'intermediate measures' are only valuable in so far as they really are relevant to the behavioural goal of sales; and in evaluating campaigns, as in planning strategy, it is essential to keep this ultimate objective in view at all times.

So, sales effects and consumer effects are best seen as complementary, not as alternatives. They give us different kinds of information. They can also be mutually supportive; and each compensates, to some extent, for the other's limitations.

Relating advertising to sales

The problems of relating advertising to sales, once thought by many to be insuperable, are principally as follows:

1. Sales are influenced by many factors other than advertising, so the relationships aren't always clear
2. Sales effects may become apparent only over the longer term, while advertisers want short-term indications whether the advertising is effective.

These are real issues, and they can make it difficult to estimate advertising effects fully or precisely; there are however ways of approaching them. But perhaps one should add a third, which I have never seen explicitly mentioned but which should be discussed before the others:

3. Many advertisers don't have good enough sales data to start with.

To look at advertising effects on sales, you normally need something better than just 'ex-factory' sales (though these also have their uses). You want a robust measure, broken down by month or even week, of what the consumer is actually buying, not what is moving into the distribution pipeline.

Many of the 'contaminating factors' that supposedly obscure advertising response – the economy, weather, seasonality, etc. – generally influence all brands on the market alike. It's therefore normally easier to see a relationship between advertising and share, than between ads and absolute volumes or values. For this, you need a measure of total market sales as well as your own.

And (with respect to Rosser Reeves' marketing men over their five-Martini lunch) most short-term variations in share, apart from those caused by advertising, can be explained by movements in distribution and relative price.

It is in any case very dangerous to look at volume sales or shares as a response to advertising, without taking price into account. Very often, the real business justification for advertising lies not just in increasing or maintaining volumes, but in maintaining a price premium; the importance of margins to profitability is often more crucial than volumes. Any analysis of sales response, therefore, needs to consider prices as well as volumes.

So in order to look for meaningful relationships between advertising and sales, you would ideally want :

- regular, reliable data on *consumer* sales of *all* the brands in your market;
- price data;
- measures of distribution.

In other words, the information you'd expect from a retail audit. (We'll leave out here any discussion of how reliable retail audits are.)

Now, many advertisers don't have this sort of information! In some cases it's available, but they can't be bothered to pay for it. In many other cases, such data does not even exist. Outside the field of packaged goods, it's probably the rule rather than the exception that robust measurements of markets can't be had, or are incomplete.

Does this mean that sales are an impossible measure after all, for those who are not privileged to have complete data? No – but it's an inescapable fact that the more data you have, the more possibilities you have both for precision, and for disentangling complex situations. Sales modelling, for instance, is not an option unless you have a fairly complete data set.

Advertising evaluation is the art of the possible. In a very dynamic situation, you may not need very sensitive data to see a relationship between advertising and sales.

If, however, you are looking for more subtle short-term movements, it stands to reason they won't show up without fairly comprehensive data. And, very important, the

---

Clarks Desert Boots

Clarks ran a campaign for their long-established product, Desert Boots, in the British 'style' press. With a media budget of only £30,000, it clearly wasn't an option to spend any money on research. Nevertheless, a convincing case was made for the effectiveness of the campaign:

- Ex-factory sales increased over 500%.
- Price and distribution remained largely unchanged.
- A 'no-cost' telephone survey of stockists and a review of advertising-related PR added corroborative evidence that the advertising had made the difference.

Source: *Advertising Works 5*

---

fact that they don't show up on inadequate data cannot be used as evidence that the advertising is not effective. It is not unknown for advertising to be blamed for what is really an inadequacy in market measurement.

If the sales data available is genuinely inadequate, it will inevitably throw more emphasis in the evaluation process onto consumer responses. But it will not make them any more of a substitute for sales data than they would otherwise have been, and their limitations in this respect still need to be remembered.

Whatever you *do* know about sales should always be compared with other sources of data to ensure it is consistent with the overall picture you are hoping to build up. If advertising measures like awareness and liking are looking good, but your own sales are down, you want to have a theory why. Is the advertising at fault, despite some encouraging, but possibly irrelevant, measures? Or is the advertising itself being received as it should, but other factors causing sales to go down? Each of these possibilities would lead to quite a different set of actions.

But the more relevant sales data you have, the more you can do to address the first issue: disentangling the effects of advertising from other marketing factors.

Looking at sales data

This begins with visual inspection of the data, relating advertising timing to fluctuations in sales or share. Despite the other factors involved, this often shows a relationship when things are changing quite fast.

The relationship then needs to be criticised by looking for, and disposing of, alternative explanations – so, comparing the sales graph with price or distribution movements, or other changes that were known to have taken place.

An unplanned experiment

Kia Ora, a fruit drink, was relaunched in the UK with a high profile advertising campaign and a complete change of packaging, from small glass to large plastic bottles.

The increase in sales was substantial – but it was not clear how much this was due to advertising or to the packaging change.

It turned out that, due to initial constraints on production, for several months independent grocery stores could not be supplied with the new packs. Special analysis of Nielsen data showed that these stores enjoyed the same increase in sales as others, and that therefore advertising rather than packaging was the driving factor behind the brand's success.

Source: *Advertising Works 3*

Visual inspection may give us a reasonable idea that advertising is having an effect, but it is not always very good at putting a value on it. To do this (and to be more certain the effect really exists) we need to have an idea about what would have happened without advertising. Often the real justification for advertising is not so much to do with a sales increase, as defending existing business – so the hypothesis has to be that sales would decline without advertising, and might only remain static, or even decline less, with it.

There are two ways of estimating this 'might have been' scenario.

Area tests and controls

The first, which has been used for a long time, is to compare sales in areas with and without advertising (or with different weights of advertising). This can be criticised as rather crude because it depends on the assumption that the two areas are similar in all other respects, which is rarely true. Nevertheless, it is still used, and the results can be convincing, though the problems of measuring and interpreting results are sometimes only discovered after the 'test' has taken place.

Econometric models

The second approach, which has become much more current in the last 15 years or so, is the application of sales modelling (also known as 'econometrics' or 'econometric modelling').

An econometric model is basically a formula which sets out to explain, or at least describe, variations in a particular line of data: this 'dependent variable', for our purposes, would most likely be a brand's market share or sales. The modeller calculates how the brand's share varies in response to other factors which data exist for, such as relative price, competitive advertising, or the brand's own advertising: these are called the 'independent variables', or sometimes, 'explanatory variables' because they seek to explain the movements in the brand share. The modeller produces a formula which attempts to predict what the brand's share should be, given any combination of values for the explanatory variables.

Anatomy of a model

Most econometric models look something like this:

$$S = K + aP + bD + cA$$

Those who are comfortable with maths will see at once what this is getting at. For the rest of us, a brief explanation should make it clear.

Each letter stands for a number.

S might stand for 'sales', or for 'share'. This is the *dependent variable*, the value which the model is attempting to predict.

P stands for some measure of price (such as our brand's price indexed on the market average), D for some measure of distribution, A a measure of advertising input . . . these are some of the many possible *independent* or *explanatory variables*. In this case, if we know the value of these three for any point in time, we can use the model to estimate what S ought to be for the same period.

a, b, and c are the numbers we have to multiply each of the independent variables by to relate them to S. These are called the *parameters*.

K is a *constant*, just a number which we have to add to the rest of the right-hand side of the equation to get the right fit with the thing we are trying to explain.

The modeller has three main tasks:

- To choose which independent variables will best explain S.
- To establish the value of the parameters and of K .
- To ensure that the relationships are meaningful according to statistical tests and to common sense.

These three tasks are all inter-related, and all involve marketing judgement as well as statistical expertise. Modelling is not (or should not be) a black box; it is an art as well as a science.

This formula can be used in various ways. It can be used to estimate what would have happened if things had been different – for instance, if the brand had not advertised, how much less its share would have been. (In the above example we would just change the value of A and see what happens to S). This offers a very precise estimate of how much extra sales can be attributed to advertising, and so can be related to profit and loss accounts.

The model can also be used to predict the future (making certain assumptions), or estimate what future shares would be given different levels of price, advertising etc., thus helping with future budget planning. One shouldn't get too carried away by this – predicting the future is never *that* easy – but in practice the results of using a sound model are generally much better than guesswork.

Good modelling is a combination of intuition, common sense, trial and error, and a thorough immersion in the relevant statistical theory. This last requirement takes about five years to master and should dissuade non-econometricians from trying to do it all themselves. The process is not, however, a black box, and a good econometrician should be able to explain most of their thinking to the non-expert.

There is not room in a short chapter to do much more than recognise the value of modelling, which I believe will become an increasingly important element of advertising evaluation. It is not, however, without its limitations. In general, models can only 'explain' things within the limits of what has already happened – so they are less reliable when factors such as price differences or advertising budgets move outside this previous range. And by their nature, models tend to explain short-term variations in the data. A model may show why share moves up or down a point or two from month to month, but not why share stays around the 20 per cent mark rather than 15 or 25. As a result, when advertising is acting over the longer term to maintain brand share around that level, the model may effectively *understate* the effects of advertising. The results of taking this literally can be disastrous. Today's econometricians are working to find ways around this problem, although the underlying issue, stripped of its modelling terminology, is simply that we do not know what might happen to a brand over the long term without advertising, unless we try the experiment. In the meantime we need to remember that what a modeller calls 'advertising effect' may not be the total effect of advertising.

Sales effects: Summary

1. Always make the attempt to relate advertising to defined sales or business targets.
2. Get the best data on all aspects of market performance that you can.
3. In particular, consider price as well as volumes.
4. In dynamic situations, sales response to advertising may be fairly easy to see.
5. Econometric modelling can be used in less obvious situations, and to put a more precise value on advertising (but is not infallible).
6. There is no easy answer to measuring 'long-term effects' in the short term – but some consumer measures may be 'leading indicators'.

The usefulness of measuring consumer responses to advertising

By 'consumer responses' I am thinking of consumer knowledge, beliefs, attitudes or behaviour that can be measured using survey research, or investigated qualitatively.

These consumer responses can be further subdivided into:

- Advertising related.
- Brand or other consumer related.

Advertising-related responses

The easiest types of 'effect' to relate to advertising are questions that find out about consumers' reactions to the advertising itself. Did they notice it, or read it? Did they remember it? What did they remember about it? Did they understand it or like it?

Recognition, or 'reading and noting'

The earliest form of advertising research, other than coupon response, was a measure of ad readership devised by Daniel Starch in the early 1920s (and still used today). This involved taking consumers through an issue of a publication they had read, asking which ads they had noticed and which they read the copy for. This tells us something interesting about an ad – its ability to attract attention – but it doesn't go very far. (It also turned out to be subject to some error: people would sometimes imagine they had noticed an ad for a product that interested them, when in fact they hadn't.)

Recall

So a more exacting test of ad effect was devised by George Gallup, which asked people to *remember* (not just recognise) which ads for a product field they had seen. Ever since, asking various forms of recall question has formed one of the staples of advertising research. It is easy to do, it gives a good spread of results, and it seems intuitively likely to most people that remembering an ad should be a necessary precursor of its effectiveness.

In general, this intuitive view is probably not too far wrong (although we can find examples from both psychology and advertising that suggest advertising can work without being consciously recalled). But some care is needed. An ad that is better recalled is not necessarily one that is more effective in influencing behaviour; retention in the memory is only one factor contributing to effective advertising.

There is another danger here, which is also relevant to other types of question asked by survey research. Any advertisement realistically addresses a limited number of the people who have the opportunity to see it. The most extreme example is the classified ad (or many retail ads) which only require a few individuals, or in some cases only one, to see

---

Sales without salience?

Eurax, an anti-itch cream, was advertised for the first time with a modest budget of £250,000. On a tracking study among all women, spontaneous brand awareness and advertising awareness remained less than one per cent. On such measures, the campaign appeared a complete failure.

However, sales of the brand increased by two-thirds in the quarter following the advertising, and combined with a price increase annual revenue for the brand owners went up by 41 per cent. Other factors were involved, but some rudimentary modelling suggested strongly these were not enough to account for the growth.

The two findings are not in fact inconsistent. Eurax was a small brand – the extra sales represented about 140,000 packs. Even if each of these was bought by a different woman, this represents only half of one percent of the population.

The use of a mass market tracking study may have been inappropriate for a brand on this scale.

Source:O'Malley, 1991

---

the ad and respond to it, in order to be a success. At the other extreme, even the most mass market products only advertise to a part of the population. Most products fall along a spectrum between these two extremes.

Where ads are addressed to a relatively narrow target audience, therefore, recall (or other) measures based on a broad sample of the population may be largely irrelevant.

In practical terms, this stresses the importance of basing any advertising consumer research on a sample that represents, as far as possible, the target audience – something that is by no means always done. But in many cases, especially if the target audience is small, this may be very difficult to do without biasing the research. We just have to bear in mind that to measure *numbers* of people recalling the ad (or the brand name, or the message) is not necessarily an indicator of the *strength* of the ad's influence on the individuals who did respond to it in some way.

Content recall, attitudes to ad

As well as measuring ad recognition or recall, surveys can ask about message recall, comprehension, or attitudes to the ad (e.g. liking, irritation, usefulness etc.). Such questions promise useful diagnostic information about reactions to the ad, and the appeal of asking them on a tracking study is that it measures response in the 'real world', rather than a laboratory situation.

The answer is 42

When we are told the percentage of the population who claim to recall advertising for a brand, it is sometimes difficult to know what to make of it. It may be higher or lower than the figure for competing brands, but is this just because they have spent more or less money? Or were they somehow more famous to start with?

To answer such questions Millward Brown developed a modelling technique that explains such a number as a combination of three things:

- the effect of advertising in the current period
- the effect of past advertising
- a base level to which advertising recall declines when there is no advertising at all (people often think famous brands have been advertised recently, when they really haven't).

This produces a value they have called the Awareness Index, defined as the amount of extra recall that will be created by 100 ratings – so the creative effects of different campaigns can be compared, independent of their weight and timing.

This helps us make sense of advertising awareness data. There is still room for debate, however, on how such a measure relates to advertising sales effectiveness.

However, unless recall of the ad is particularly high, this can be a difficult and expensive method of finding how people responded to the ad. If, on a sample of 500, only 10 per cent remember seeing it at all (not a very low figure), this leaves only an absolute maximum of 50 who can then be asked more detailed questions about it. So despite the artificiality of the viewing situation, a great deal more diagnostic information can be gathered more cheaply by using some form of 'impact and communication' test. This kind of research is useful as part of a campaign tracking procedure, as well as in a 'go/no-go' pre-testing situation.

Brand-related consumer responses

These are most commonly:

- Brand awareness, spontaneous or prompted.
- Brand image or perceptions (i.e. a range of attributes).
- Overall attachment to or rating of the brand.

Brand awareness

Brand awareness is always easy to measure, but not always very relevant. For some situations, spontaneous awareness is important – I have a need, I think of a name in response to it, and the 'salience' of one brand name over another gives it a greater chance of getting the business. In these cases it is also important to specify the correct 'trigger'.

The appropriate trigger for brand recall

A US Brand, Liquid Plumr (a product for unblocking drains), defined their competitive set as not just other drain-cleaning products, but all drain-unblocking services.

The appropriate question to measure salience of Liquid Plumr was therefore not:

'What drain cleaning products can you think of?', but:

'What would you do if you had a blocked drain?'

But in many other cases, spontaneous awareness is not so obviously important. In a lot of purchases we are choosing from a range of alternatives displayed before us, not searching for a name we have already thought of. It is true that in most such situations, even if we know nothing much about the brands on offer, we normally tend to choose one we have heard of over one we have never heard of.

When brand awareness is important

When buying a life policy or pension through an independent broker, a customer is offered a choice of two or three brands which have already been objectively selected, by the broker, to suit their needs. It is therefore very difficult for them to make a further selection on 'rational' grounds.

Research showed very clearly, however, that people would always choose a familiar brand over a less familiar one. For Scottish Amicable it was estimated that if advertising could increase prompted name awareness, it would lead to an increase in acceptance and so in sales.

A new campaign in 1991 increased brand awareness from 40 per cent to 60 per cent with a resulting 15 per cent increase in sales.

Source: *Advertising Works 7*

For established brands in big markets, however, prompted awareness is not a very useful discriminator as the figure is likely to be above 90 per cent.

There is, to confuse the matter a little more, also some evidence that the ability to think of a name spontaneously is an indicator of positive feelings about the brand. But not infallibly so: we can all think of very famous names which are famous for negative reasons. If this is the purpose of the questions, therefore, we need some more direct evidence of brand attitude as well as mere 'top of mindness'.

Brand image and attitude

There is no room in this chapter to describe the range of techniques that exist, qualitative as well as quantitative, for attempting to measure the beliefs and associations of various kinds that consumers may have for different brands, and which I still prefer to lump together under the overall name of 'brand image'. Nor the equally wide range of approaches that can be taken to measuring overall brand attitude or 'brand strength'.

The relevance of these kind of measures, and the exact formulation of them, should depend on the kind of mental process by which advertising is expected to work. Some campaigns are intended to influence behaviour by communicating information, or by changing the context or associations people have for the brand. Questions can be designed to check whether these communications have been effective. In other cases, advertising may work by reminding them of things they already know, or making the brand name more top of mind; here, brand image type measures may not be very relevant to advertising effect.

There are two general points to be made that apply to this kind of measure. One is the effect of brand size in making sense of the data. The other is the frequency with which these things need to be monitored.

The brand size effect

This is most simply illustrated by an example:

	Cornflakes	All Bran
Q: Which of these brands would you say tastes nice?	64%	10%

It would be easy, looking at this, to conclude something like: 'Cornflakes is obviously a stronger brand than All Bran on "Tastes nice". There's a clear goal for advertising to persuade people that All Bran tastes as good as Cornflakes'

But what in fact happens is that bigger brands in a category (which essentially means brands bought by more people) tend to get rated more highly or on more attributes by more people. Such patterns therefore don't add anything much to our knowledge that Cornflakes is a bigger brand than All Bran.

	Cornflakes	All Bran
Tastes nice	64	10
Easy to digest	60	19
Popular with all the family	61	5
The kind you come back to	65	4
Reasonably priced	59	5
Average	62	9
Buy regularly	48	7

(abridged from Barwise and Ehrenberg (1985))

This pattern doesn't explain away all the variation in the data (if it did, the survey wouldn't tell us anything useful). But what is significant is the way that individual figures differ from what would be expected: e.g. All Bran is clearly higher than expected here on 'easy to digest'. There are various ways of looking for this: by graphing, or by looking at how each figure varies from the average. Another approach is to analyse perceptions by users of each brand.

This 'brand size effect' is fairly well known, but it has a further implication for advertising evaluation. If a brand's share goes up, we'd naturally expect to see more people rating it on image attributes. To see these figures move up doesn't necessarily tell us much about advertising effect. If, however, the brand moves more strongly on some dimensions than others – say, something featured in the advertising strategy – it adds to the evidence that advertising was influencing the sales movements.

Tracking studies: how often do we need to measure change?

The type of questions described in this section are perhaps most familiar today as constituting the ingredients of 'tracking studies'. This name has been used to describe any research repeated over time, whether the interval be annual (or even less), or weekly, as in the continuous tracking studies that have become popular in recent years.

Different frequencies of conducting research have different pros and cons. For monitoring advertising response, annual (or even quarterly) surveys have disadvantages – they may fall shortly after or a long time after the last burst of advertising, making comparisons of the results over time almost impossible to read. Because of this 'pre and post' surveys are more often used, where timing draws a clear contrast between the before and after, or ensures that waves of research are at an equal distance in time from the advertising.

In many ways, therefore, the ideal would be a continuous tracking study which monitors every peak and trough of response; many very clever things can be done with continuous tracking studies. But they are extremely expensive, requiring huge amounts of fieldwork – apart from possibly using up a disproportionate share of the research budget, this cost factor can easily lead to compromise on length and quality of questionnaire. To measure brand image sensitively requires in most cases a longer questionnaire than is possible on the average continuous tracking study.

It also happens that measures of brand image, if they are meaningful, generally move rather slowly – in fact, the only type of consumer response that consistently moves rapidly and in obvious response to advertising, is advertising recall. It is therefore questionable how cost-effective it is to monitor brand image or brand attitudes on a continuous basis. It might be more sensible in many cases to conduct a more in-depth study of brand perceptions and usage, every year, or even every other year.

The question of how often to 'track' responses to advertising needs to be considered individually for each case, taking into account how quickly relevant responses are expected to change, and how much money is realistically available for the task. If the price of continuous tracking means that the brand will have to do without reliable market data or sales modelling, or proper in-depth understanding of consumer usage and attitudes, it is probably not worth it.

Claimed behaviour, and other questions

In some cases tracking studies, or 'pre and posts', need to include questions about usage of the product because reliable sales data don't exist. Asking such questions can also tell us who is buying what (not apparent from the normal retail audit), and is in any case needed in order to cross-analyse the data by brand usage, etc.

Claimed behaviour may go beyond simple purchasing. It may be a way of estimating new trial, if that was the objective. Sometimes advertising works by encouraging a particular type of usage, such as the Hellmann's Mayonnaise campaign.

So such questions are often important, even though we know that claimed behaviour is generally less reliable a guide to actual behaviour than panel data.

Changing usage behaviour

Prior to advertising, mayonnaise was seen by the UK consumer as a dressing for salads, which considerably limited its potential for growth. A new campaign for Hellmann's based on the line 'Don't save it for the salad' encouraged usage in many other situations, leading to a trebling of the mayonnaise sector over three years. One measure of advertising effect was the number of consumers using Hellmann's in ways other than salad.

Source: *Advertising Works 3*

Consumer response: Summary

1. Measures of advertising recognition and recall can be useful, but despite their popularity they are not measures of advertising 'effectiveness'.
2. In-depth information about advertising response may be more cost-effectively gathered in a laboratory-style test than in a tracking study.
3. 'Intermediate measures' should be selected to fit our expectations of how the advertising should influence behaviour: e.g. by factual communication, or name awareness, or imagery.
4. Measures of brand awareness are sometimes highly relevant, and sometimes largely irrelevant, depending on the nature of the purchase decision.
5. Numbers of respondents rating a brand on any attribute tend to vary with the brand's numbers of users, and this needs to be taken into account when interpreting the data.
6. Brand image and attitude tend to move slowly, and an in-depth study every year or two may be more valuable than the attempt to track continuously.
7. Claimed behaviour is useful either as a surrogate for proper market data, or to measure other aspects of changing behaviour, or as a cross break for analysis.

'Indirect' effects of advertising

Everything written so far is implicitly about the 'direct' effects of advertising on the consumer. But it is important to remember that advertising often works in other ways, by influencing employees, the retail trade, or journalists. The significance of these effects is often ignored, but they must be taken into account when evaluating a campaign.

A note on consumer panels, and 'single source'

Consumer panels to some extent straddle the two categories of 'sales' and 'consumer'. Panels are often used to monitor aggregate market share data and can provide much the same information as a retail audit, including price, though not distribution, and therefore can be analysed or modelled in a similar way.

But they also provide information not available from a retail audit. They can measure, for instance, levels of trial and repeat purchase, and patterns of brand switching, all of which might be very relevant to evaluating certain campaigns. They can also tell us who is buying, or among what demographic groups sales increases are happening.

There has been a lot of work done recently in the USA and in Europe on 'single source' panels; these are panels where both purchasing behaviour and media exposure are measured for the same sample of respondents (Jones, 1995). As this is expensive and difficult to do, a practical alternative which is also available is to produce a similar database by 'fusing' together a separate purchasing panel with a media exposure panel, such as AGB Superpanel with BARB. In both cases, this offers the opportunity to relate ad viewing to brand choice at every level from the individual upwards.

The apparent potential in single source panels for a new, more precise and informative means of evaluating sales response to advertising has excited a number of people. However, the sheer quantity of data that such systems create, while tantalisingly offering the answers to many problems, makes the best mode of analysis a far from straightforward matter. The area is currently, therefore, somewhat dogged with controversy which there is not space, nor perhaps a pressing need, to enter into here. For our immediate purpose – which is a brief practical guide to techniques readily available today – we may conclude that at the time of writing, 'single source' is still at a somewhat experimental stage as a practical tool for advertising evaluation. Proper single-source panels are immensely costly, and are therefore not easily available, though fusion may be a way of getting round this. While all this may change, single source is not at present the Holy Grail of advertising research, whatever its enthusiasts may say.

Conclusions: putting it all together

As we said at the start, there is no single simple and reliable way to measure advertising effect. The best approach is to measure more than one level of effect in order to build an overall picture of how consumers are responding to a campaign. This should always involve looking at sales, as far as possible, as well as different measures of consumer response (and being alert to indirect effects as well).

The secret of campaign evaluation is selecting and designing measures which reflect the objectives and the strategy of the campaign. If the objective of the advertising is essentially maintenance, or price enhancement, it is pointless to look for short-term leaps in volume; there is no reason why a niche brand with a one per cent market share should want to double its spontaneous awareness among a broad target market of all category users. It is a matter of thinking, not of applying universal formulae; apart from certain pitfalls which are not obvious (the main ones being mentioned in this chapter), advertising evaluation does largely depend on imagination and common sense.

To end this chapter, and pull together some principles already suggested, I describe an outline review process recently introduced into DDB Needham around the world. It is called the Evaluation and Learning Process: because ultimately, the most important purpose of evaluation is learning for the future.

Evaluation and learning process

What did we expect to happen?

Be clear about what this particular campaign was meant to achieve, and how we expected it to work:

- Overall business objective, e.g. maintenance, growth, price, quantification.
- Target audience.
- Desired action – where in the purchase decision process did we want to influence their behaviour?
- How the advertising was expected to influence them: e.g. awareness, fame, attractiveness, information.

What did happen?

Review the best evidence we can get about what happened:

- To sales.
- To the consumer.
- To other parties (retailers, competitors).
- And what else was going on in the world: new products, the weather, health scares etc.

Isolate the effect of advertising from other factors

Does it look as if the advertising worked?

- Then: are we confident it was the advertising and not something else?
- Play devil's advocate!

or,

Does it look as if the advertising didn't work?

- Were the objectives unrealistic?
- Did other events interfere with what we were trying to do?
- Or was the advertising at fault?

Diagnose reasons for failure (and for success)

- Strategic reasons: e.g. wrong choice of target audience, misunderstanding of consumer motivations, buying decisions, etc.

- Executional reasons: ad not linked with the brand name, alienating people, misunderstood, etc.
- Media/ budget: outspent or simply not spending enough

<u>What have we learnt from the experience?</u>
<u>What should we do next?</u>

Open-ended questions!

At this point, I cannot improve on the concluding line written by my predecessor in the earlier version of this book, because it is logically inescapable:

'Go back to Chapter 1.'

8 Account planning and media planning

'Maids of honour and cooking eggs'

Dan O'Donoghue

Introduction

The purpose of this chapter is to stress the growing importance of account planning and media planning working closely together. At a time when scent is sprayed from posters, station departure boards show brand symbols and even petrol pump handles are used for advertising, the two disciplines most closely associated with the planning of advertising effect need to work together and to prepare together for a more complex future.

Some years ago I stopped off in Madrid together with our French planning director, Marc Loiseau to obtain the co-operation of our Madrid agency in using a common approach to the briefing of creative work. We had a set presentation that lasted about two hours and ended with an example of a briefing format. Arriving at 11 o'clock, we presented our thoughts to a gathering of the great and the good in the agency boardroom which went fine. At lunch time we were to discuss implementation with the account planners. Would we be speaking the same language?

The core media channels

Our objective in choosing the right medium for creative work must be to produce a connective effect between our target audience and our message. The viewer or listener or reader must be drawn into the dialogue that we are trying to achieve and if we do not capture their attention then we are not likely to produce an effect. The various media available to us differ quite widely in how we interact with them.

Figure 8.1 is a simplified view of some of the differences between media. The 'Budget Issues' and the 'buts' have to be weighed against the benefits of the stimuli and the job the advertising is trying to do. In general the more stimuli the better the impact.

Television

Television has for a long time been the pre-eminent medium as far as manufacturer brands are concerned. It can give you quick access to large audiences and offers vivid colour, sound and movement. People feel television is important to their lives. They

	Television	Cinema	Radio	Press and magazines	Outdoor	Internet
Stimuli	Words, colour, music, movement	Words, colour, music, movement	Words, music	Words, colour	Words, colour, limited movement	Words, colour
Budget Issues	High entry cost	Expensive	Cheap	Variable costs but easy to buy	Expensive	Cheap to try
Media Planning Issues	Dramatic, important and influential but difficult for small targets	Even more dramatic than TV but slow coverage build	Can catch people 'in situ' (e.g. driving) but limited coverage and station demographics differ widely	The most personal medium but regional variation and low impact	'Loud' and quick but research limited so far	The most trendy. Conversational in tone but tiny penetration

Figure 8.1: Some differences between media

learn about the great events of their lifetime, the excitement of sporting achievement. They can follow their own lives written into soap operas and they feel that everyone else sees these things too. It is still the important medium and has the lion's share of media attention because it is so glamorous. It is our main connection to the world at large and its great strength is its ability to get hold of the emotional side of our brains with music, movement and colour. This is a powerful help to achieving share of mind and, if the task is to elbow other brands out of people's affections, TV usually gets the vote.

Posters

The poster is still the only medium that offers no competition for the viewers' attention but the advertisement itself. It's just there to be an advert! For this reason it has the potential to be a strong primary medium for brands and not just a back-up to other media. It is a highly 'public' medium – part of our daily environment whether on the side of a bus or round a football field. Its nature is for the message to be short and the branding to be large. If it is well used it can be the most talked-about medium. Several brands, for example Silk Cut, Orange and Perrier, have used the medium to dramatic effect. But it is difficult to be emotional with posters. As a stand-alone medium (and often seen from a car) the message has to be instant, though it can be subtle. At its best it can create the feeling of 'something happening' by virtue of it public siting, which is why it is popular with politicians. The value of a good poster campaign can be disproportionately higher

Visual 8.1: Perrier advertisement

than other media because of this 'in public' nature. Nowadays moving posters, painted buses and 3-D specials add to this effect.

Radio

A large amount of radio advertising is for retailers, local businesses and for promotions. That is not to say that it cannot be used for brand building. Listening to radio often accompanies other activities be they driving a car, making a meal or hanging out in your bedroom away from your parents. These are often marketed as segments, e.g. a drive time schedule. Radio is a very personal medium and one that is interacted with in a routine manner – people listening at set times of day every day and every week. Recent developments have seen the establishment of some national elements in the radio mix like network chart shows, classical music stations and talk shows, and increasingly the playlists of pop stations are nationally sourced to provide a more cohesive national audience. Briefing radio campaigns needs special effort given the wide variation in audience by station and the difficulties creative teams seem to have with the medium. The Radio Advertising Bureau[2] whose job it is to promote the medium are an extremely helpful source for both data and stimulus material.

The press and magazines

The press medium is, a mass of slightly different publications and a comprehensive list is available in BRAD.[1] The main distinctions in print media are between news media, leisure media and special interest media. News media like national newspapers can be considered as a 'badge' that agrees with your personal view of events. Thus new newspapers find it hard to establish a position as most of the political stances have been taken. Leisure media, chiefly magazines, tend to take 'lifestyle' or 'mindstyle' stances – healthy, sexy, liberated, sporty, home loving and so on. New magazines tend to be launched to capitalise on new 'stances'. Special interest media (of which there are thousands) from

The Loss Adjuster to *Croquet News* to *Farmers Guardian* have an avid but necessarily specialist and small readership.

Thus the press is a very personal medium and each editor will have a very definite picture in their mind of the type of reader they are appealing to. Co-operation with print media to understand the readers in more detail is relatively easy to organise via your media planner.

The daily press is thus typically used for 'news' advertising messages, be they retailers or financial companies telling you about their latest offers or brands adapting their campaigns to fit some topical theme. This is an area where close liaison with your media planner can bring some exciting opportunities to stand out. Magazines, being read more for leisure, tend towards personal advertising messages like clothes, beauty aids and perfumes.

In trying to build brands in print media, advertisers often use the press as a 'mini poster' medium. This makes use of the fact that press and magazines have a much larger readership than purchase – some magazines being read by up to 20 people and lying around for up to six months, and not just in doctors' surgeries! Given the amount of commercial messages that consumers are subject to, long copy ads have an increasingly difficult job to achieve stand out. Increasing the page 'environment' is being used to add substance to the brand message – for example always placing vitamin ads on the sports page or water ads in the top person's recruitment section.

Visual 8.2: Vittel advertisement

Cinema

Cinema appears to have everything a medium should have. It has sound, colour, music and movement and a dramatic large screen. The audience is usually young, upmarket, captive and in a good mood! But cinema is a special occasion treat. For a young audience this could be as often as once a week but on average it is a lot less frequent and for that reason it takes a long time for each individual to see the advertisement several times. Thus a cinema advertising brief needs to take this *infrequent viewing* into account.

Cinema, of all the media, illustrates the point of having the media planner in the same room as the creative team when discussing the brief. How the creative work could interact with the medium can be a potent help to your brand's campaign given the infrequent visits of your audience. British Airways even went to the effort of employing a person to sit in selected cinemas and answer back to the screen. The dramatic and public relations effects of this can add considerable value to the media spend

The Internet

A currently nascent and small medium but one which is growing in importance.

With the internet you have to actively become involved in the medium. That's the whole point of it and why it is so different from all the other media. The effect of the Internet is in some ways similar to radio in the 1930s. It speeds communication over large distances previously unthought of. We will no longer be left to potter along and wait for the latest fashion to happen in due course. We will know about it in seconds, and, unlike radio, we can see pictures and hear sound. Despite all the technology, the medium itself is conversational in tone, even more so than the press. It is worldwide but one to one.

From an advertising point of view you have to search out the advertisement. Thus the advertising has to reward you for your search. A recent example of a Guinness TV commercial being made available as a computer screen pagesaver downloaded from the Internet led to thousands of computer screens showing the commercial in businesses all over the UK. Despite its infancy the Internet is very interesting as a medium because of the dominance of computers in schools and universities and their strong interest in certain categories. For example the Euro '96 site achieved eight million visits.

It is clear that the press medium will be affected by this development and already several newspapers are experimenting with on-line versions of their product. World-wide web numbers on your ad are becoming *de rigeur* if you want to be young and fashionable.

Figure 8.2 is a simplification of the roles of the account planner and media planner in debating the relevance of various media

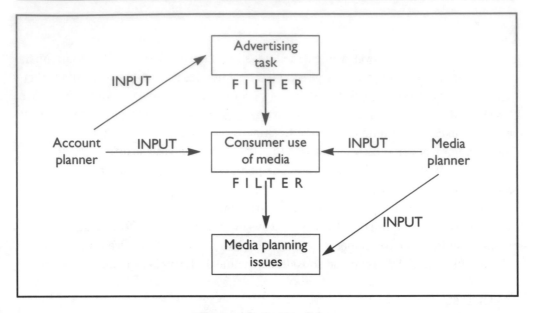

Figure 8.2: Work flow

Modern problems

The modern media scene is just not simple any more! Figures 8.3 and 8.4 show how media have exploded since 1975. The modern media planner is faced with an ever-expanding fragmentation and segmentation of media that at first sight easily explains why media experts are needed more than ever. In 1980 there was one commercial channel in the UK; in 1995 there were 46. To cope with this there are now electronic links between all the major UK TV sales points and the large media buying points via a system called NOMAD.

Segmentation of media enables special interests to be catered for more regularly. Sky Sports for example enables more specific targeting to sports fans. Segmentation like this enables segmented brands to use media like TV that might otherwise be unaffordable. Fragmentation, however, is a big problem for the media planner. Despite the hugely increased availability of airtime on TV, viewers actually spend slightly less time watching TV and the percentage watching the 'big' regular programmes has gone down significantly. Thus the definition of who you wish to reach with your advertising, and how often, becomes vital.

In 1975 the average adult was subjected to about 300 commercial messages a day but by 1995 it was 3,000. Nowadays one-third of homes have three TV sets and around one-fifth cable or satellite. Four out of five have a video and one in three a computer. These are now serious competitors for the average person's viewing time. Figure 8.7 shows the expanding media supernova.

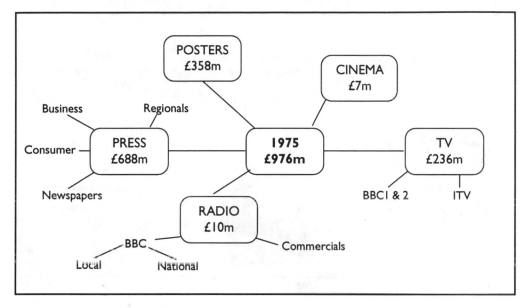

Figure 8.3: 1975 'traditional' media landscape

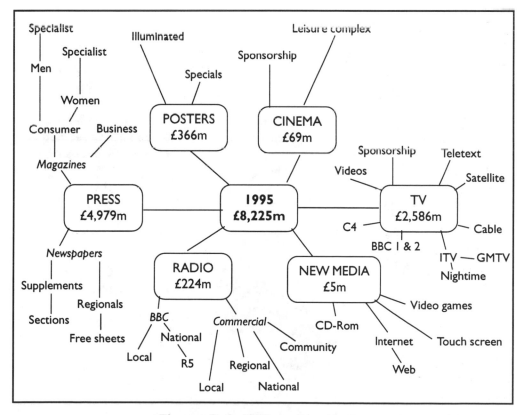

Figure 8.4: 1995 media explosion

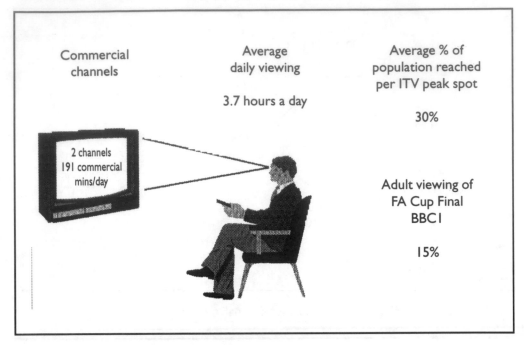

Figure 8.5: Audience fragmentation on TV 1985

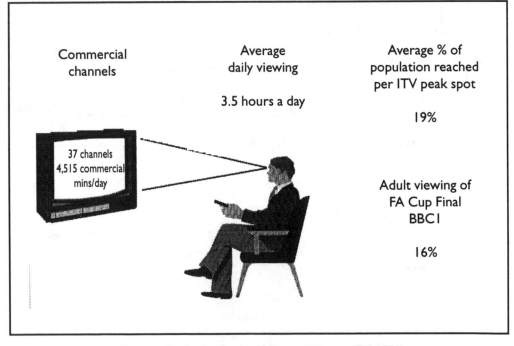

Figure 8.6: Audience fragmentation on TV 1995

Increases since 1975

Newspapers	+ 4 titles, sections and supplements
Magazines	+ 4,500 titles
TV	+ 46 channels
Radio	+ 150 commercial stations
Outdoor	+ specials, illumination
Cinema	+ 460 screens, leisure complexes
New media	Home PCs (30%), Internet, CD-Roms

Figure 8.7: Media explosion 1975–95

As a consequence of this the modern media planning world is far more technically complex than it used to be and an awareness of how media planners approach their planning is more important than ever.

Unbeknownst to us Spanish lunch started at about 4 o'clock – and so to fill in time and to try to get into a Spanish frame of mind, Marc suggested a quick trip to the Prado to see Las Meñinas. Las Meñinas (The Maids of Honour) is a quite extraordinary painting by Diego Velazquez. It captures and holds your attention for minutes on end. In fact you find it quite hard to leave its presence. It is almost the size of a 32-sheet poster and the images in the painting seem to somehow know that you are watching them . . . and they are watching you. A seventeenth century Madrid court scene caught in an exact moment of time past. Looking at you, in the present. One character in particular held my gaze for a long time. A small child. A girl with a strange face – more adult than child and dressed in an elaborate and fancy dress. The dog in front of her, who appears half sleeping, seems to be her guardian as she stares questioningly at the viewer. If only she could talk! The language of Spain . . .

Understanding the language of media – the media brief

The media brief should be the formal summation of the advertising task that the media planner will take on to a solution. It should also contain as accurate and helpful description of the target audience as we can achieve. Figure 8.8 is a fictional example of a progressively tighter description of the target audience changing the media solution – with money ignored for once! It shows how more definition by the account planner can widen the options rather than close them down.

In writing a media brief the account planner should be aware of the background to a media planner's thinking in suggesting alternative media. In the evolution of media

Target audience considerations	*Media solution*
16–34 adults. National. Crowded competition.	**TV** 80% of the audience covered in four weeks. BUT
Distribution is in high street shops *only*. Target is mainly in conurbations.	**Superlite posters** Concentrated in urban areas targeted to distribution patter. BUT
Average purchase interval is four days and loyalty to existing brands is strong. Young people 'wear' their soft drink. 16–24s are more important as they keep the habit in their 20s.	**Radio** 73% of 16–24s in four weeks but can afford a long duration. Can incorporate sponsorship and promotion/phone-ins. Sampling opportunities at summer events. BUT
In product tests the product appearance was key to trial (it has an unusual appearance).	**Press and magazines** Can be tailored: inserts and free offers. Magazines are very personal. Sold at soft drink point of sale. BUT
Consumers are bombarded with competitive ads in all these media. Women are much more important than men in terms of purchasing.	**Cinema plus Internet** Audience matched to films that women prefer. Promotions tied in to cinemas. Competition to win free Tilt on Internet and get 'night out' with Rod Stewart on World-wide Web.

Figure 8.8: The launch of Tilt carbonated drink (fictional). *Source: Optimedia UK*

Client	Brand	Date
Budget	Campaign: Start	Finish
(Media only, specify net/gross etc.)	Schedule to account Management	
	To client	Approval

1. **Background** (Indicate if new or existing campaign, include key creative considerations)

2. **How is the brand bought?**

3. **Key market factors** (e.g. seasonality, regionality, distribution, competition: attach if required)

4. **Advertising objectives**

5. **Target audience** (Demographics and any relevant attitude/psychological info.)

	Strategic planner	Account director	Media planner	Creative director
Signed				

Figure 8.9: Media brief

departments into modern media specialist companies the major driving force has been the development and evolution of the media's power.

As media has formed itself into ever larger and more international power blocs so media companies have grown to balance the buying and selling power equation. The media planner now has two quite clear and distinct roles to fulfil. One is to satisfy the efficiency needs of buying media competitively and the other is to satisfy the effectiveness needed from media solutions. These two needs are not necessarily easily compatible and the modern danger is that they are not even considered as different. The media can be bought cheaply but there may be little effect of the creative message. If this happens we divorce the medium from the message.

Media functions

Planning:
- Assessing the target audience in media terms.
- Choosing the medium/media.
- Assessing the efficiency of the media plan pre- and post-activity against standard media surveys.

Buying:
- Buying the media efficiently, i.e. achieving a competitive rate for the target audience. Some media planners will also be buyers of media though TV buying is usually separate. Buying is a highly complex and competitive task akin to a dealer on the stock exchange.

Research:
- Providing research to enable the planner to consider intra-media choice for a given target, e.g. *Sun* vs *Daily Mirror*.
- Providing research to enable the buyer to get the best rates from the medium, e.g. although the *Express* is good for young upmarket urban men it has a low percentage of buyers of Brand x. Therefore its rates are too high for Brand x.
- Providing TV rating[2] data to assess different programmes.
- Developing research to produce better methods of maximising the effect produced by the medium, e.g. qualitative research reveals some men read newspapers from the back page, breakfast TV watchers use the medium like radio, magazine readers always eat and drink while reading, etc. How can we use the creative idea to maximum effect using this knowledge?

The media planner takes the target audience from the media brief and uses it in two ways. The qualitative definition and the advertising objectives aids the choice *between* media and the standard demographics are used to evaluate the efficiency of how the chosen medium can best deliver the audience.

The trip to the Prado had been an inspiration. Now we were to have a 'close liaison' with the account planners over lunch. But then it all started to go complex. Post-Franco Spain was in turmoil. No one wanted to talk about Velazquez or Las Meñinas. In our enthusiasm we had misunderstood politeness for agreement. 'You do not understand the new culture of Spain and its new advertising. Your briefing would be too rigid. It is not our language. We cannot work with such a system!'

Some thoughts on what should be included in a media brief. It is worth remembering that the language of media is technical but down to earth. Psychology is less useful than in a creative brief.

Background

The background section should inform the media planner of marketing or advertising issues that affect media choice. It may be that the previous medium did not produce the desired effect. The new creative work may have particular devices suited more to some media than others. Direct response may need to be measured and the telephone number important to register. Be direct if you have evidence.

How is the brand bought?

How the brand is bought is a seminal issue that should inform all subsequent target audience debates. It is also a difficult question to answer. Is it an impulse purchase? Is the purchase interval three years or every day? Where is it bought? Is it asked for? Do you have to fill in a form to get it? Does a salesman call? Do your parents recommend you? *Where could the advertising fit in to a model of purchasing and what effect could we reasonably expect it to have?* If you can provide a good analysis of the purchase process this can be crucial to good media choice. Try to buy the brand yourself or observe the process at first hand.

Market factors

Media planners need to know about seasonality and regionality because media markets and therefore media prices are seasonal and regional. TV prices are cheaper in January and in the West Country. Quite often competitive dominance of certain media, seasons or regions will also influence planning. These issues weigh heavily in media planners' minds because of the important cost implications.

Advertising objectives

The advertising objectives will necessarily be the same as for the creative brief and should be stated as simply and succinctly as possible. If the objective is awareness raising but because of the budget or target audience TV or posters are unaffordable then the media planner may have to think of more creative ways of using other media. It is useful to state objectives in non-'marketing speak' and avoid jargon. Be clear.

This is where the interaction with the creative team is key. In practice it is often best to discuss the creative and media brief in draft form first with creative and media before finalising what is agreed. This enables a more expansive discussion to take place before things are set in stone.

Target audience

Given that you have isolated how the brand is bought and whether it is the buyer or user you are targeting then there is usually some quantified data to enable you to give a good picture to the media planner. The picture given may vary in its ability to replicate media survey data like the Target Group Index3. The account planner may be working with an extremely detailed knowledge of both the demographic and psychographics of the key audience but the media planner has to translate this into audiences that can be bought demographically. TGI data is thus worth sharing.

Media buying performance is measured against limited standard demographics. Some audiences are easier in some media than in others, e.g. young upmarket men are not an easy TV audience. Thus agreeing what is a sensible target audience and how it can be described is vitally important.

A useful tip given to me by a media-turned-account-planner is to find an example in the medium that seems to sum up the target audience: a particular TV programme, magazine or radio show. Whilst qualitative in nature it can help the media planner see the picture you are trying to paint. The written media brief is a great help to media planners but is is a complement not a substitute for conversation and co-operation.

Campaign evaluation

Campaign evaluation is an ongoing task with three basic areas for evaluation:

* Efficiency of the campaign (TV) as measured by standard media surveys like BARB.[2]
* Effectiveness of the campaign measured by:
  - 'Intermediate' surveys on awareness, attitudes and claimed purchase. These surveys are called intermediate measures because they measure claims by the public rather than actual behaviour.
  - 'Direct' measures such as sales or advertising response, e.g. coupons returned.

Efficiency measures

Efficiency measures are the preserve of the media company and the client. They measure how well the buyer performed against the average. This can be translated into a notional cost saving compared to the average cost of a TV spot or the quoted price of a half-page press advertisement. Thus the buying efficiency of the media company is assessed.

Traditionally a media planner will start with a budget and determine what this will buy in terms of coverage[2] and frequency.[2] If, for example, 80 per cent cover of 16–34 AB women is needed how many OTS (opportunities to see)[2] do I get for the budget in this medium. If this seems too low they can then play around with the coverage figure to get what will seem a reasonable frequency given the duration of the campaign. There are various computer programs to help them do this quickly so that they can consider many options.

Effectiveness measures

Intermediate measures

These are most often tracking surveys and are carried out by large research companies on large samples of the target audience. They include measures such as recognition of the advertising in addition to awareness of the brand. It should be remembered that it is possible to have good increases in awareness of the advertising but little or no effect on the brand. In such cases it is necessary to carry out some diagnostic work on why this is the case – usually qualitative research but also looking at media factors. Maybe share of media voice (SOV),[2] is lower than last year. Intermediate measures are important signposts to advertisings effect but short term fluctuations should be treated with caution Year on year comparisons are a minimum for safe analysis.

In measuring short-term effects on advertising awareness the timing of the media spend and its relation to the fieldwork dates is important.

Some recent work on effective frequency linked to sales results by J. P. Jones (1994) and C. McDonald (1996) has caused some rethinking about the planning of media. Put simply, the effect on the media planner is to ask him/her to start from the question of 'What frequency do I wish to achieve?' If, for example, the planner takes the view that the frequency target should be one OTS per week (i.e. that is what appears to have the greatest effect) then he will have a very different campaign length than if he is trying for four OTS. The account planner needs to talk to the media planner about their planning philosophy as the evidence piles up that 'How often for how long?' can affect the short-term results in a relatively dramatic way.

Direct measures

In measuring direct effects of advertising the account planner should be able to feed back to the media planners all the issues that can effect sales other than simply the advertising weight – distribution changes, promotional impact, variant launches, price fluctuations and competitive impact. This will enable a more sensitive evaluation of direct effects to be made. For direct response campaigns the timing of advertising and the link to response mechanisms are an art in themselves. How many phone lines are we setting up? When will they be manned from? How will each advertisement be identified? This can be time-consuming to check but worth the effort.

Things were looking difficult . We had made little progress as later that night we trooped through the Plaza Mayor in the old town to a place where Flamenco dancers performed and everyone ate tapas. We discussed the centrality of snacks to Spanish culture as the dancers pounded away. 'The music of persecution.' Why did you go to the Prado?' murmured the Spanish Planning Director.

'To understand something of Spanish culture,' I said. 'With old paintings?' he replied.

'It is only the modern that ever becomes old fashioned – as Oscar Wilde used to say,' was my final riposte.

Conclusion

The modern (or should it be modem?) media world is vast, complex and exciting. Interactivity, media creativity and media tone of voice are current buzzwords and putting a telephone number on an ad can be more about extending the medium's effect on brand recall rather than simply building mailing lists. Modern media planners want to achieve stand-out and integrate with the creative idea. The account planner wants the advertising to be effective with the target audience. These two objectives need to be integrated for optimum results for the advertiser.

The role of the account planner must be to try to bring the creative and media people together by using the briefing process to maximum effect. By using the planning skills of analysis and interpretation she or he can spark the reaction from the colleagues to produce the great idea, brilliantly executed in the media. Get to understand the media language and culture a bit more. It's the best place to start.

Outside the Flamenco club it was snowing. Snow, in Madrid, in April!! We shivered in our lightweight jackets. 'You know,' said the Spanish planning director, 'you should go to see the paintings Velázquez painted in Sevillá, when he was young. The old woman cooking eggs, for example. The paintings of optimism.' The Spanish Planning Director was from Seville . . .

'I will,' I said. 'I will use the brief, then.'

9 International account planning

Rita Clifton

A double page ad with the headline 'The Opportunity for World Brands' appeared simultaneously in the *Sunday Times* and *New York Times* on 29 January 1984.

In it were the main arguments for why the globalisation of brands was not only possible for today's ambitious companies, but essential to long-term survival and profitable growth. It provoked a very public discussion about the extent and desirability of international brand marketing.

However, there were no mentions of globalisation, or even 'international' in the last publication of *How to Plan Advertising*.

It's not difficult to understand why

First, the truth is that 'globalisation' was still something of an experimental science in the mid-1980s.

With the honourable exceptions of Procter & Gamble, and of the American Dream brand exports like Coca-Cola, Marlboro and McDonald's, the vast majority of companies were still in fragmented Export Department mode on the international scene. As Andrew Seth, former CEO of Unilever put it, 'We got used to overstating the case for globalisation because if we didn't, the issue would have been marginalised.'

Also, as a discipline, account planning had not been very successful at exporting itself at the time of the 1987 publication. Of course there were 'International Account Planners', but invariably based in the UK and often having to spend their time either analysing international market models, or generating research evidence to show that 'internationally developed' advertising treatments were not appropriate for the sophisticated British advertising consumer. As with the old Export Departments and international account handling, the international end of planning tended to be tarred with the attitude of 'the door only swings one way'.

The situation is startlingly different in the late-1990s.

Campaigns which have some international application are estimated to make up 50 per cent of today's advertising business. Something like 70 per cent of advertising reviews with significant budgets involved are now conducted regionally, not nationally. Most agencies have been subject to 'international realignments' – for better or worse.

Unilever has recently been reported to be culling up to 20 per cent of its weaker (i.e.

smaller and less profitable) brands to concentrate its power brands and resources for global competitiveness. Doc Martens is suddenly a global player.

Account planning is really becoming established internationally – in particular after stutter-starts in the US in the 1980s. UK planning directors are increasingly being asked to take on pan-European management roles for the discipline. And while this doesn't mean there's a will or a budget for a classically trained planning department in each European office, it does mean that head-hunters are as busy trying to fill planning slots on accounts with an international dimension and across European offices, as they are on local business.

While companies will continue to make adjustments to optimise how their own global brand marketing is done, business, market and consumer factors will ensure that the trend will not be reversed. The reasons will be discussed later.

All in all this means that the demand for planners with an international perspective will continue, and that there is indeed a robust case for devoting a separate chapter to the role in the APG book this time around.

What is international account planning?

Inevitably, people use the term 'international account planning' rather loosely – as indeed they do the terms 'globalisation', 'international' and 'multi-national', not to mention recent self-conscious inventions like 'glocalisation' and 'multi-local'. For the purposes of this paper, we should probably define *global* as being the approach that starts out with the intention of standardising as much as possible across as wide a geographical area as possible. An *international* approach would be less ambitious, but would still seek to take a common perspective across markets. A *multi-national* approach is one where the main thing in common is company ownership, with perhaps just a sharing of insights and information on a co-operative basis.

Like international brand marketing, international account planning can range from the sharing of information and insights to help one or two European markets develop their own campaigns, to being the central strategic thinker on communications for a consistent brand spanning 60+ markets.

For this to be a 'How to do international account planning' guide, it is tempting to write 'Just apply the previous eight chapters only do it bigger.' Clearly, the discipline of planning is the same whatever your geographical stretch. However, you will almost certainly need more flexibility and more stamina. You'll need the patience and personal authority to make order and inspiration from what is often chaos. If you're an obsessive perfectionist or purist, you'll hate the messy bits of markets that don't quite fit your clustering, and you'll get exasperated by the number of people who won't play ball for protectionist or macho reasons.

International planning can be like a kaleidoscope or hall of mirrors on people, brands and company cultures. It's your task to help clients look beyond corporate dogma and strategic neatness on globalisation/localisation. In particular, it will be your primary task to help clients (and agency people!) concentrate on what touches the people that really matter – i.e. their *customers* – rather than their internal processes and politics. Otherwise, it really will be an impossible mission to achieve effective and efficient marketing communication on any international stage, let alone advertising that you can be proud of.

The rewards can be excellent – both practical and emotional. If you are truly interested in the human condition, and on a grand scale, the excuse and opportunities for exploring people and cultures on a profound level are always there – both in informal and formal research. And corny though it might sound, it's quite extraordinary seeing people from more than 30 different countries and cultures being moved by a central creative thought you have helped inspire (as in the case for the British Airways 'Global' commercial, for example).

So get your symbolic passport ready. We will now look specifically at some of the theory and practice of this relatively new role. Remember, there are almost certainly even fewer 'right answers' on the international planning scene than on local discipline. Each agency and each planner will have different tools and approaches, and this will change over time to reflect the flux of client business.

So basically read, think and then do your own thing.

The development of international marketing

At one end of international marketing, the argument for globalisation goes something like this:

1. Companies need profitable growth.
2. Being a dominant brand and a low-cost producer is key to this.
3. Static, mature markets cannot deliver enough growth and further economies of scale.
4. You need to find new markets.
5. Leveraging existing product, research and marketing costs makes sense and delivers economies.
6. Consumers are converging demographically and attitudinally to allow a common approach.
7. Sell to them properly and you've got an increasingly successful (and profitable) global brand.

To quote the original Professor Theodore Levitt article on 'The Globalisation of Markets' (*Harvard Business Review*, 1983):

> 'The globalisation of markets is at hand . . . The global corporation operates as if the entire world (or major regions of it) were a single entity: it sells the same things in the same way everywhere. '

Well, it is certainly true that the effects of 1992 (remember those endless presentations on 'What'll happen post the liberalisation of European markets'?) are really being felt in British business just about every day now and GATT will certainly facilitate the original theory.

However, initial reports on the imminent death of multi-national practice and mentality turned out to be rather exaggerated. Companies who over-enthusiastically embraced economies of scale, and too rapidly went the whole global hog – from product to positioning to strategy to creative execution – found themselves without enthusiastic eyes and ears on the ground to drive local business and initiatives. Also, they found themselves with the sort of bland wallpaper communication that international committees could have been designed for – 'style videos' masquerading as ads for goods like soft drinks, cosmetics and toiletries, and watches.

The trade-offs could be summarised as follows (Figure 9.1):

Figure 9.1

More specifically, you could list the 'pros and cons' of global standardisation, and see the *extent* to which each balances the other in each case (Figure 9.2).

Pros	Cons
Cost savings/economies of scale in production, packaging and communications	Local needs sacrificed to lowest common denominator
Pooled budgets means potential better quality marketing mix	Temptation to be cost-driven versus consumer-driven
Smaller countries get access to higher-worth thinking (and production)	Temptation to 'force-fit' solutions
The brand is consistent in overlap media areas, and to international travellers	Local gaffes more commonplace
Ability to 'deal' on regional/global media opportunities	Potentially less responsive to rapidly changing market needs

Figure 9.2

Inevitably the balancing of central strategic control and local motivation has been preoccupying major corporations. As Peter Brabeck-Letmathe (CEO-elect of Nestlé) has said:

> Food is extremely local. If you try to be too global you lose efficiency in communication. I am struggling to prevent us oversimplifying our world.

Nestlé should know – while they have worldwide corporate brands like Nestlé, Carnation and Maggi, they have over 7,000 local brands.

Perhaps you could map your own existing or prospective clients on the following scale for corporate culture and organisation, e.g. 'centralised' would be a company like Rolex, or British Airways (see Figure 9.3).

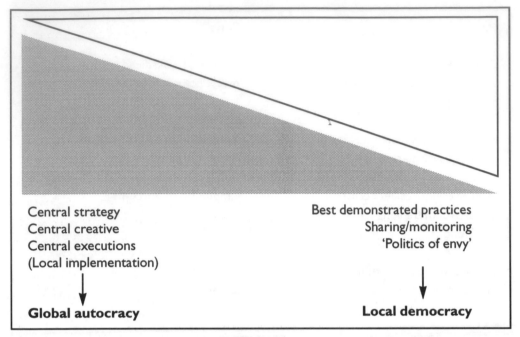

Figure 9.3

Most companies are now clustering around the 'middle line' anyway, i.e. global/international strategy, energetic local input and tactical implementation. The trend towards globalisation is tending to be not so much a straight line development as a progressive 'learning loop', or sometimes a 'nice pendulum'. As the Chairman of Nestlé USA said on this subject:

> 'Try to envisage a continuum between centralisation and decentralisation, then imagine there's a dot on the continuum that is constantly searching for the point of optimisation. The environment is changing fast, so we must keep adjusting to be efficient.'

Frankly, there's little option but for agencies and planners to swing with it.

The most visible issue in globalising or internationalising brands is still whether and how much the packaging and advertising actually looks and feels the same. The obvious question is . . . well, *should* it, *could* it be the same, from the perspective of *real people* and how *they* are changing . . . ?

Where does international account planning come in?

It's probably no coincidence that the consumer factor came in at about number six in the 'argument for globalisation'. We should remember that most internationally ambitious companies go progressively global for *business* reasons, and 'because they can'. There was no initiating consumer will out there to buy standardised global brands.

The international account planner has a key responsibility to bring the perspective of real people in to every meeting; to make sure that international marketing communication decisions are connected to what enough people want to think, feel and buy – in any country.

Despite an unpromising consumer starting point, there are now burgeoning reasons to begin your international consumer investigation with 'Why should these people be different?' rather than 'These people cannot be the same'. We *can* see the same demographic patterns in western markets, i.e. more practical and social mobility, more working women, 'maturing' populations, higher divorce rates, higher living standards and aspirations.

Media convergence is obviously both a major influence and facilitator of cultural convergence. Television has been coined the Third Superpower, while media companies themselves like CNN are now truly global brands. On a different note, you can draw your own conclusions from Baywatch currently being the most-watched television programme in the world.

Now clearly, global media channels (including the Internet) and rapidly increasing foreign travel give the most extraordinary opportunities for global harmonisation of brands and communication – as well as providing an extra 'stick' for companies to harmonise. Otherwise there is the potential confusion for travelling consumers who may wonder why an invigorating, energising drink in their own country is sold as a bedtime snooze-inducer elsewhere (as in the case of Horlicks).

The convergence opportunities (and imperatives) are heightened further when you focus on particular target groups: *business travellers,* for instance, who have international frames of reference anyway, and show very similar discriminators for travel choice worldwide; *teenagers* across the world who will share musical tastes and fundamental characteristics like 'rebellion'; cross-cultural interest groups like *sports* enthusiasts, *surfers, bikers, environmental activists.* These are people that we could accurately describe as 'global tribes', who will see common media, and enjoy common experiences – physical and emotional. What sense would it make to fragment the targeting of these people by geography?

The important thing for the planner is, no matter what the *channels* of communication of today and the future, the critical part of the role will stay the same, i.e. to inspire the kind of creative ideas that break through information overload, and touch enough of the right people to make a client's business viable – wherever it is in the world, and whatever size.

Despite the tide towards more standardisation and globalisation at the top end of business and consumer trends, people will also talk about the polarising forces at the local, grass roots end of consumers and communities. People's 're-discovery' of local, cultural and regional roots is probably almost inevitable as a corollary of the globalisation of life otherwise, and the symbolic, if not literal, destruction of national barriers.

Of course, there will always be local opportunities for authentic brands. However, even brands that start out as local, community, 'cult' brands (e.g. Ben & Jerry's and

Snapple), can now be flashed onto the international stage as soon as they are seen as successful, and if they can continue to feel authentic on this broader stage.

Historically, people have viewed food and drink as the most difficult categories to 'internationalise', since their usage is so deeply tied in to a culture's tradition. However, you need only look at worldwide food brands like Del Monte, Buitoni and McDonald's, and to know that it was possible to sell bottled water to the British and breakfast cereals to wider continental Europe, to know that anything is now possible. There really are few sacred category cows any longer. These days, look for similarities and you shall usually find.

The issue is, *how* to do it, and how international account planners might practically go about it.

Throughout the next section, it is as well to bear in mind the words of Confucius:

'In terms of human nature, people are much alike. But in terms of practice and effort, they are quite different.'

The practice of international account planning

It's just worth emphasising that the following is not intended to be a re-hash or summary of the previous chapters. It is rather to look at what we would see as the particular requirements and differences in planning with an international dimension. It is also working on the assumption that your *client's intention* is to find as common an approach across markets as their business organisation or culture will allow.

1. Getting your bearings

One of the hardest things to get to grips with when you first start working on an international brand is how to get the main points and shapes of the problems, opportunities and issues into your head in a memorable form. Before you get too heavily involved in the process and history of the account, you'll find one of your best investments and allies will be a simple matrix-type chart (no matter how big!), which summarises basic market and consumer information, by country. The matrix shown is a suggested start (Figure 9.4).

There s no point in pretending it's going to be easy to get this data in some markets, and from some clients (some of whom will be wondering why you want business data when the 'agency's just there to produce the advertising'). If nothing else, the exercise will highlight for you just how much or how little comparable data there is – and how much you might need to recommend setting up yourself. In the meantime, there are three ways you can tackle this:

* Engage the client in a persuasive 'in order to make the advertising as relevant to your business needs as possible, we've got to understand your business'-style conversation.

	Markets	1	2	3	4	5	6	7	8	9
The brand										
Market size, volume and value										
Market growth last five years										
Market sectors										
Year brand launched										
Brand shares top five brands										
Growth of our brand										
Distribution										

	Markets	1	2	3	4	5	6	7	8	9
The consumer										
Market penetration										
Brand penetration										
Profile of market/brand users										
Psychographic profile										
Usage habits										
Brand image										
Local idiosyncrasies										

	Markets	1	2	3	4	5	6	7	8	9
The advertising										
Media spend, category and by brand										
Share of voice										
Positioning										
End line										
Any competitive positionings										

	Markets	1	2	3	4	5	6	7	8	9
Summary										
Strengths										
Weaknesses										
Opportunities										
Threats										

Figure 9.4

- Set up your own consumer omnibus-type research to get basic comparable data on who uses what in which markets; or
- Get the data by more indirect means. If your agency has an international network, obtaining basic data will at least be feasible. However, you will almost certainly have to push for facts and hard numbers – either because they are genuinely not available, or because they're a hassle to get. Be absolutely specific in what you're requesting.

If you really have no other consumer data to go on, think about sending a questionnaire to the (non-involved) people at some of your key international offices, or asking them to do some interviews to get some kind of international comparisons of brand usage and saliency. Although purists might be fainting at this point, it's better than absolutely nothing.

You'll often find that international media owners are veritable mines of information – ask your media-buying agency to get the information you need. Just be aware that the data the media owners produce will, not surprisingly, be geared towards selling airtime and space to people like your client. so you should tend to look at numbers relatively rather than in absolute terms. Also, ask international research companies for any feedback they might have on your category, brand and potential consumers.

What I'm suggesting overall at this stage is that you try to take a first, objective overview of *what* seems to be going on and *where*, and to see any obvious clashes and groupings. For instance, if your brand is sold on the basis of superior quality in one market, and family value-for-money in another, you'll know you've got a challenge on your hands. However, now you've used primary data sources wherever possible, you can start getting to the bottom of *why* all this is happening, and seeking more involved views and opinions. You'll find that your initial 'objective' exercise is even more critical in international account planning because not only will you get your fill of free opinions and secondary data all too soon, you must also be careful that you are not bringing your own (national) prejudices with you about the brand.

Make sure you look at all the historic advertising for the brand and its competitors. Look for any patterns that may or may not be intentional, like tone of voice, personality, as well as the main selling ideas.

Finally, note down all your hypotheses *now.* Can you group some markets together in terms of:

- Are there any *obvious* reasons that your brand is more or less successful in each market? Me-too product or positioning/indistinct positioning/particular targeting/wallpaper advertising/strong, new and/or focused competition?
- Which markets seem to be new, developing or mature? Group them by this, and by their relative success/growth priority, perhaps as in Figure 9.5:

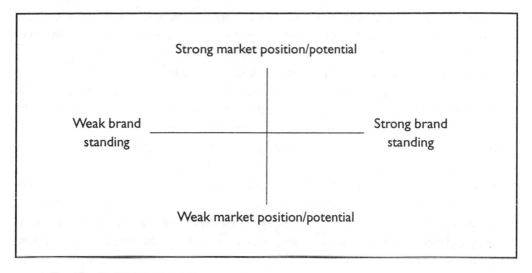

Strong market position/potential

Weak brand standing

Strong brand standing

Weak market position/potential

Figure 9.5

This grouping might at least help concentrate the mind for the next stage.

• Are there any advertising approaches that seem particularly strong for you, with selling ideas that stand out (whether for your brand, or the competition)? These might well be useful for the strategic research stage.

2. Understanding the task

Unless you happen to be working for a client who is at the extreme 'global autocrat' end of the spectrum, in which case the task should be clearer, you will need to think about applying planning principles to your client and agency populations too. With international business, it is critically important to elicit the range of your clients' views up front.

As part of your familiarisation with the business, or even if you say you want to take a fresh look at the business, find out:

a) which clients will play a role in the final decisions on the advertising;
b) who else at the client end could have a particularly useful contribution to developing the substance of the brand and communication strategy (e.g. product development people, research directors, sales force, etc.)?

. . . and arrange to see them, preferably on their home territory, so you can take the opportunity to get direct experience of their market, culture and *modus operandi*. An example of this still haunts me. On a new business pitch once, when we turned up at a company's head office, there was a notice just above the stairs saying 'Please take the steps one at a time'. This should have told us something about the company culture! The advertising solution we offered them was in retrospect far too daring and racy.

Understand the company culture as you would do your consumer – if only to ensure that if you feel you need to sell a provocative strategy, you will know how to present it in a way that they can listen to.

Suggestions for your informal 'discussion guide' would be:

- What would they see as being the main strengths and weaknesses of their brand in their market? (Prompt with market, product and consumer.)
- Has the brand been as successful as it might have been, in their view?
- What do they feel have been the main reasons for its success and/or limitations?
- What do they see as the main business objectives for the brand: a) within the next year, b) in two to five years' time?
- If they had to sum up in two or three words what the brand stands for now, and what they feel it will need to stand for in, say, three years' time, what would they be? (Probe why.)
- Who do they view as their main current and future competition?
- Any strong views about the strengths and weaknesses of the brand's current and previous advertising? Any competitor's advertising they particularly admire and why?

It is often useful to summarise your findings, and feed this back (without attribution if appropriate) to your client group. Not only will it be valuable to you as brand and cultural background in its own right, it will also help to highlight genuine differences of opinion and areas of debate which otherwise may have stayed hidden until you presented the advertising! Additionally, it may well give a great basis for you being able to justify some up-front, detailed strategic research.

3. Developing the strategy

Right, you've done your collecting, listening and initial hypothesising. Hopefully, you are able to group markets in some way – whether by stages of market development, brand maturity and/or positioning. The important thing now is to see whether, and how, there might be common nerves to touch – across how many markets and, potentially, when.

Your 'audits' will be good evidence for the need to do some common strategic research. I cannot emphasise enough the importance of doing this exercise up front. We all know how hard it is to get agreement and hold to a written creative brief amongst a national team. The relationship between clients and agencies around the world will tend to be much more based on 'Do we like the advertising/storyboards when we see them?' It will only be when people actually see pictures, videos, lines and ideas, that reality will bite. It is a much better use of resources and everyone's sanity that potential routes are explored strategically, than via six finished creative ideas to six different strategies.

So, how do you get to these strategies? Well, you may want to see how far you can go with the following in common:

'Brand territory'
i.e. what the *main brand property* you want to own might be, e.g. 'health', 'refreshment', 'naturalness', 'freedom', 'sensuality', etc . It 's important to try to get this focus, because just having a set of 'international brand values' will tend to result in flabby international advertising.

Substantiating 'facts'
i.e. product/usage facts, phrases, insights that will anchor the brand territory, and will help people believe. Also, these facts will later provide the basis for stronger creative work based on a *product truth*, which will travel better, rather than user imagery stereotypes, which will not.

Brand personality
One of the most difficult areas to pin down internationally. But it's important to try to get a common feel for more emotive and indirect aspects of the brand's personality – for instance, which senses, images and colours come to consumers' minds, as well as the usual 'living personality' analogies like kindly doctors, scientists, James Dean and Arnold Schwarzenegger (if you insist).

You can obviously develop these hypotheses, options and source material in a variety of ways:

- A spectrum of ideas coming out of your initial brand audit/trawl.
- Trawling for common popular films and magazines amongst the target groups and which might be relevant to the brand's area (e.g. we found the film 'Wall Street' represented a common myth of 'corporate skulduggery' across our business groups in the 1980s, just as American 1950s films and soundtracks represented strong shared myths for teenagers and Levi's).
- A collective brainstorm with a spectrum of international client and agency people across boundaries. This is thoroughly recommended, providing you have the final edit on output, and get a research company on board to support you in limiting the options! It's also a great way of 'selling' your planning input and facilitation skills to a spectrum of clients, several of whom may still be wondering what planners really do.
- A 'semiotic' analysis of the category in some key markets, to get at further cultural triggers and clues. This involves looking at the broader cross-cultural background and context for the category and brand.

What you are trying to get to the bottom of at this stage, is the *potential* for bringing a brand together internationally – either now or at some point in the future. Or how far along the spectrum of commonality you can legitimately take consumers, and when. For instance, it's interesting that Timotei is sold on the basis of 'outdoor naturalness' where the rural idyll and blonde naïvete are highly evocative in urbanised Western countries, whereas in Thailand images of 'country' tend to signal backwardness and deprivation, and were inappropriate. One just has to accept that different economic cycles and centres of young population growth can fundamentally affect the brand, and disallow a 'same time, same message, same everywhere' approach. This is not to say the brand can *never* be brought together internationally, and that at least a logical pattern of brand development should be followed. The convergence trend mentioned earlier will either mean an accelerated cycle to Western values or, as many predict, Eastern values will increasingly influence Western societies. Either way, it will be an eventual convergence.

4. Doing the research

The first thing you may feel with doing any research on an international basis is that someone's put the noughts in the wrong place on the cost proposal. Some countries are still exceptionally expensive.

The critical thing is to choose a research company that you feel understands you and the task, and has enough stature and maturity to understand the politics of international marketing companies.

It's obvious to say that clarity of the research brief is even more critical internationally. Clear objectives and an *explicit* description of what you want as output/use of the research are essential, as is the list of all the questions you just know the client in France is going to ask. Also, make suggestions for stimulus material at this stage. Tools that tend to travel are:

- Bubble diagrams.
- Collages/words and pictures.
- Psycho-drawings.
- User imagery.
- Video clips.

Provisionally choose representative markets from across the 'segments' you made earlier, i.e. take a 'mature' market, an emergent one, ones with currently very different brand positionings, if you are genuinely trying to see the possibilities for eventual convergence. Sampling can be a bit of a nightmare – not only in theory, but also in practice in markets like Russia. All one can say is, be as specific as you can be if it really matters – for instance, with style leaders, and with (truly) frequent business travellers. Ask the research companies to specify how they'll find the right people.

Get proposals from your candidate companies. Choose these on the basis of 'I really like working with these people, and they have offices in other countries' *or* 'These people look and sound OK, and they happen to have an affiliate in the country I really need'. You'll be amazed at how many research companies *say* they're international, and actually do Europe, the USA and Japan if pressed. Worry if they don't make a real contribution to your ideas for stimulus material, and/or don't include interesting cultural insights based on their previous experience with this category, market or consumer. They don't have to be experts in NLP or anthropological scholars, but it might help.

Better to have a great researcher than a great linguist. Ask how they might explore getting to the *deepest emotional trigger* in a category (in our experience, the best and indeed only place to start if you're aiming for a common approach). Essentially, ask how can they get at the deeper-seated emotional needs and truths that your brand might commonly satisfy? We have often found 'laddering' to be a useful way of getting at this, as in this example in the PC market:

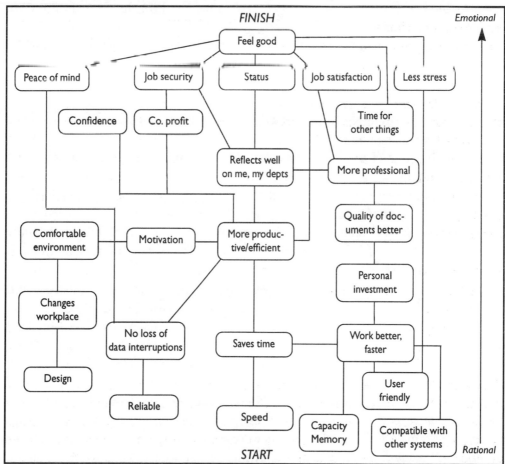

Figure 9.6

This laddering analysis will give you the full range of possibilities that your brand might enter on.

Ask how the research company co-ordinates its projects. Does someone (you meet) go out and brief their affiliates personally? Do they see all the groups? Beware the 'phone and fax' school of international research if texture and detail is important to you (as it almost always is).

When you have selected the agency, or had it selected for you, try to make sure a fair selection of the appropriate clients (or their representatives) are at the briefing. A good research company is a critical ally in helping less sophisticated clients understand the value of indirect, provocative stimulus material, and the value of effect and impressions, versus likeability and opinions. This will, of course, apply even more to creative research than strategic. I remember one example where an (unnamed country) client said she wanted the idea and all the executional details checked against the original brief – from a drawn story board. The research company director tactfully asked 'But surely you want to know how people respond to the *idea*, rather than the animatic as a piece of film?' Bless that woman.

Finally, be strict about the need for *central production* of stimulus material. One of the main reasons for doing this exercise is to explore common images, words and symbols.

5. The creative brief and briefing

So, hopefully, you've had a good debrief with lots of guidance on common truths, myths, triggers and visual language. You've drafted a pearl of a brief, and used all your audits and research to get rich and simple answers to the main headings. (See Figures 9.7 and 9.8 for suggestions.)

You should have lots of visual, verbal and moving images to show what does and doesn't get the common consumer response.

After this stage, if you have several clients to take on board, you may decide you only want to agree the broad objectives of the creative brief. The reason is that, in many planners' experience, you can spend so many empty hours debating the detail, specific language, nuances, and, in particular, the proposition and mandatory inclusions, with an international client committee. All round, it would be best if all could just agree on the *main territory* you are going to try and own with the brand in this advertising, and *how the client is going to judge the success of the campaign* – in terms of consumer response and a realistic or surrogate measure of sales. Then, to agree to judge the creative work on that higher level. See what you can do.

There are a number of things to bear in mind when briefing an international campaign to creative teams from different offices – in fact, very similar to the sorts of things you must bear in mind for creative work to work on an international consumer scale. As a rough and ready reckoner, you can apply this scale to what is likely to work and not (Figure 9.9).

Client	Brand	Date	Job Title
Account Group	Creative Group	Planner	Media Planner

Why are we advertising?
(Include market/consumer/competitive situation, client objectives as relevant)

What territory do we want to own, and why?
(Include brand and product strengths and weaknesses, research indicators, client preferences)

How are we going to judge the success of this campaign? (Given sufficient weight and time)
(Include 'hard' and 'soft' measures, including sales effects, behaviour and attitude changes, other tracking measures, trade/sales force feedback, company morale and so on, as appropriate. Include those measures the client will use, and be realistic)

Figure 9.7: Background to creative and media brief

Client	Brand		Progress Controller	Date
Account Group	Creative Group		Planner	Media Planner
Job Title			Development Budget	Production Budget

	TV		Radio		Press		Poster		Direct Communication
Promotion Ideas		Sponsorship Events			In-store	New media			

Campaign requirement

Target audience. What they currently think and do

What should the advertising make the target audience think and do

The single-minded proposition

Substantiation for the proposition

Desired brand character

Mandatory inclusions

Date from client	Core group meeting	Interim review date	Date to client

Signatures		Creative services	
Group Director	Planner	Director	Creative Group Head

Figure 9.8: Creative brief

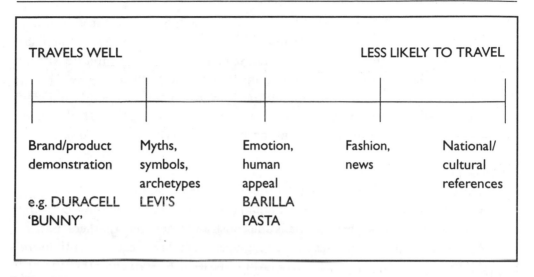

Figure 9.9

In briefing, make sure you bring the brief to life with as much visual and symbolic language as you possibly can – and as many product/factual nuggets as seemed to get an interested consumer response in research, or in your judgement.

What is also often useful in international briefing is to produce something like a compilation video, which might make the point that a lot of international campaigns in this category look the same. For instance, trawling the world for airline advertising makes you notice how prevalent are the clichéd images of planes taking off, planes flying, animated route maps to show the size of their network, champagne pouring shots, business people relaxing back in reclining seats, the smiling/fawning stewardess shot. This kind of 'same, same, same' video as briefing material will pay dividends later, as you may help the creative teams avoid the obvious mantraps-that-don't-seem-so-obvious-unless-you-know.

The trickiest areas will tend to be word-play and humour. The former is obvious, in particular if you bear in mind that the English language tends to have so many possible meanings and nuances loaded into its vocabulary; contrast this with Germany, where one word will tend to mean one thing (or rather, its range of meanings is not the same as the range of meanings of the 'equivalent' English word). Also, British humour, particularly of the self-deprecating kind, might work here and in the US, where it's thought to be quirky and cute (à la John Cleese), but will be watched quizzically by Southern Europeans and Germans, whose humour will tend to be different, perhaps more slapstick.

Finally, probably one of the worst ways to brief a great international campaign is actually to ask for a Great International Campaign. Some of the most original and successful 'international campaigns' just started out with being a great idea in one country – for instance, the Andrex/Scottex puppy, Levi's, and Guinness. Get familiar with the award-winning campaigns at Cannes. So many of them communicate with all nationalities despite their original language. And frankly, I can think of very few Agency networks who couldn't do with a better attitude towards taking successful campaign ideas from other countries and re-applying them, and without being forced to do this by their client. Great ideas are as hard to come by as ever, wherever in the world you are.

6. Evaluating the creative idea

Of course, you should evaluate and develop the creative work you see in exactly the same way as for a national campaign, i.e. as a human being first. From your knowledge and experience, apart from the obvious pitfalls and constraints mentioned earlier – is there a strong core idea that will *connect* with enough people and connect to a truth in the brand? If there are executional issues like casting, location, lifestyle clues that you just know will cause problems, would it fundamentally affect the idea to change those? Or could you do various national executions on the same theme anyway?

Be honest as well as positive. There are few things more professionally depressing in advertising than seeing an idea having bits plucked away (or added) over time until it dies of torture.

In researching the idea, the previous section covers most of the practical issues of choosing a research company. With executional, creative development research done internationally, you're likely to get into even hotter debates with your client than normal about the need for evaluative, quantitative research, rather than qualitative development. Use all the arguments in Chapter 6, and also:

- It's even more important to represent the *idea*, mood and tone as explicitly as possible. The British Airways 'Global' idea was researched by using a video clip of the Olympic Games, with the crowd forming shapes. Then, the art director's rough drawn storyboards and a 'Lakme' music soundtrack were used to explain the idea. An animatic on its own would *never* have been able to represent the feeling of scale and emotion, so quantitative evaluation on a clutter reel would have been quite worthless.
- In many countries, research is conducted in rather formal viewing facilities. Beware the client watching advertising groups unless you have been clear at the research briefing what you think will be important responses, and why. For example, many clients – not just from other markets than the UK – will expect people to *like* the advertising and be able to feed back clearly what's being communicated. During a particularly sensitive de-brief, when the research company was being very positive about the overall communication potential of an emotionally-based campaign idea, the German client burst out with 'But I watched the group for two hours, and they

understood nothing!' Remember that, as with any creative research, if any clients have an underlying worry that the creative work is wrong, there will *always* be reasons to blow it out, with the sensitive political balances often present in international advertising development making these even more possible.

It's a really critical role of the international account planner to keep people focused on whether the idea is likely to communicate the *main* thought to enough people. Keep drawing people back to the focus of the brief, and the *effect* the advertising is likely to create, versus consumer and client opinions.

7. Monitoring campaign performance

It will be exceptionally difficult to get to the bottom of what's really going on in sales terms in so many markets – and sales will sometimes not even be collected in the way that represents what the advertising is trying to do (e.g. the client might just collect sales *volume*, when you know you're trying to build the *value* and *premium* of the brand). So, to be on the safe side, make sure in setting up your brand and advertising monitor that you specify some kind of *brand consideration/brand commitment/intention to buy* scale, as well as the usual awareness and brand imagery measures. Further, make sure you collect information on respondents' *product experience*. In international work more than ever, you'll need to be able to disentangle whether advertising is doing its job of building saliency and consumer 'willingness' to develop a brand relationship, from whether consumers' product experience is or isn't helping to complete a success cycle.

Other hints and tips for travellers

There are a number of other bits of advice offered by seasoned international account planners on a personal and day-to-day working level.

Meetings, meetings, meetings

You're likely to find yourself in planes, airports and sitting in meetings much more often than you need to be. Unless you particularly love working all the time while travelling, are brilliant at faxing with your laptop, and don't mind forgetting what your home and family look like, *be firm about which meetings you really need to go to.* As a planner, you *must* have time to think and write – also, there is often only one of you, having to cover both marketing and research people at the client end, perhaps in several different markets. Enrol your account handlers in this, to help protect your time.

So, what do you do ?

Although the situation is changing quite quickly, many clients and some agencies, particularly in Europe, will be unclear as to what planners are actually there for. It's a good idea to emphasise the consumer angle of your expertise in particular up front, and to go further than you might normally do in demonstrating your 'added value' work like consumer trends, interesting ways of segmenting markets and consumers, and leading-edge use of research methodologies.

Make sure you hone your presentation skills to a fine art – it's particularly valuable for international work, and an easy way to make strong initial impressions. Accept offers to talk about what planning is, and present planning case studies. It's good for you, good for the planning cause, and good for improving the standing of international advertising all round. It all helps.

Other planners

Again, the situation is changing, but often if networks do have planners in many offices outside the UK, they might well be only working on one large piece of multi-national business, or stretched across all the accounts in the agency. Be generous with sharing tools, case studies, anecdotes and time. Remember also that this should be two-way traffic. Don't behave like an arrogant Brit, just because your department is ten times the size.

Conclusions

International account planning, like international advertising, really can and does work. You *can* help to inspire creative work so simple and powerful that it touches human beings everywhere. There's undeniable satisfaction in seeing evaluation charts like those opposite, which show just how common and powerful a response to a well-targeted ad like British Airways' Club World 'Boardroom' commercial from the late 1980s can be – despite the different countries' attitudes to the brand initially (see Figures 9.10 and 9.11).

Yes, this ad had to be adapted to show mineral water rather than wine in the Middle East; yes, the words 'Like a lamb to the slaughter' had to be changed for Muslim countries; and South Africa had to film its own version. However, the targeting and narrative format really worked on an international scale.

But don't expect to win them all. Even the British Airways 'Global' commercial, acclaimed as 'ad of the decade', failed to capture the hearts of the Japanese flying consumers in the same way as the rest of the world. In practice, it proved more effective and efficient for Japan to run their own advertising, which leads me into the final point.

In the end, the issue for this chapter is, how can you justify and make an international approach work philosophically, practically and economically. The only reason to adopt an international approach is if it *works* better, i.e. if there is to be any trade-off in abandoning a successful local strategy, this needs at least to be compensated by the economies of scale, or by likely future consumer requirements. Based on the

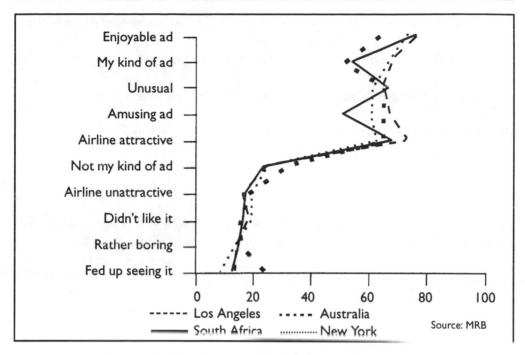

Figure 9.10: Opinions of British Airways: 'Boardroom'

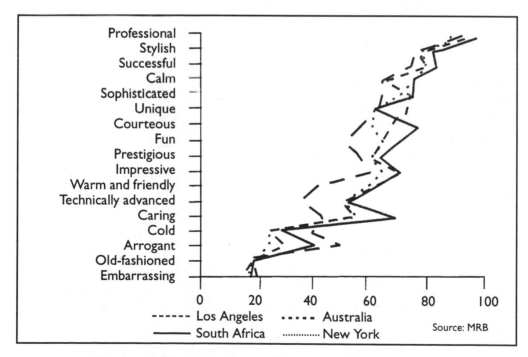

Figure 9.11: Descriptions of British Airways: 'Boardroom'

real-world evidence, what do you believe is the optimum mix of common strategy, common positioning and common execution? And how could this change over time?

As Faith Popcorn said at the end of her best-seller *The Popcorn Report:*

Questions? Thoughts? Call me. Write me. Fax me. Beam me up.

I'd now of course add 'E-mail me'. In the meantime, happy travelling, and good luck.

10 Planning inputs into the client's business

Paul Edwards

Introduction

From a client's point of view the planner is often perceived to be in a unique position of trust. The planner did not write the creative work and so is expected to be less emotional about it. The planner is not selling the creative work and so is expected to be more objective. This position of trust allows the planner the potential to get closer to the client's business than anyone else on the team. The planner therefore has the opportunity to establish ownership of the 'ends' rather than just the 'means'.

'Ends' refers to the overall objectives of brand building, creating commercial opportunities and achieving sales. 'Means' refers to advertising, promotion, direct marketing and the other tools used for communication. By owning the 'ends' the planner creates a role in which seeing the bigger picture is essential. A role which makes the planner (and their agency) a potentially indispensable partner for the client and a role which nurtures the best conditions for excellent creative input. For the planner this is the opportunity to occupy the pivotal position between the goals of the client and the agency.

This chapter aims to look at the planning role in broad terms, seeking particularly to consider the contribution of the planner to 'ends'-based thinking. It will cover the role of planner as brand champion; the contribution of the planner to business thinking; the planning of the broad communication strategy; the importance of effectiveness and accountability; and the input to market research.

Planner as brand champion

A brand is a precious commodity, its value is often ascribed to the ability of the brand to charge a price premium over lesser named goods/services or shops' own labels. Strong brands have a value beyond this as they are enduring; which in business terms means that they are a source of a long-term earnings stream, bringing income to a company potentially over decades. Both Mars bars and Kit Kats were on sale to chocoholics in the 1930s.

The golden dawn of television advertising in the late 1950s and early 1960s saw the birth period of many of today's household names. In the fragmented media environment

Date of launch:	
Before 1900	4
1900–1950	16
1950–1975	21
1975–present	9

Figure 10.1: Top 50 UK brands

which now exists, and the concentration of retail sales into relatively few hands, it is now much more difficult and expensive to create new brands (of the top 50 brands in the UK only nine were launched since 1975) (Figure 10.1). Fortunately, it is also relatively difficult to destroy a strong, long-standing brand in a short period. But it is only by careful nurturing over the long term that brands yield their full potential.

The pressures of business, particularly for stock market listed companies, mean that there are nearly always good reasons to take more profit in the current period rather than to invest in communicating the brand to its customers. The tenure of the current brand management team will often be over before the consequences of under-investment come home to roost. The planner needs to be in a position to put the brand first in order to fight the exigencies of the short term. The right to participate in the debate over investment comes only through a demonstration of intelligent argument; passion alone is no longer enough.

Other chapters in this book deal with developing strategy and using data to create advertising. The ability to marshal these arguments, to show a deep knowledge of the client's business and to present them in a concise, relevant and, preferably, fresh way are all part of winning the long-term argument.

Client companies often have access to huge amounts of data about their consumers and their markets.[1] If not, it is the planner's responsibility to ensure that relevant and actionable data are sourced. It is crucial that the planner accesses these data and knows them at least as well as the client. A command of the data not only allows persuasive and well-informed argument, but also client senior management can be impressed by such mastery (not to mention senior management within the agency who love to bask in the reflected glory of intelligence deployed on their clients' behalf). Reinterpretation of tracking data, collation of qualitative research possibly going back over several years, reanalysis, or simple repercentaging, of quantified data can all help to support the argument in favour of supporting the brand. At the same time the planner is gaining trust as a knowledgeable spokesperson for the brand. Even using the client vocabulary is a simple way of showing empathy with the business. This learning comes from regular contact with the client and not just the immediate brand management team. The market research manager will often be a crucial ally, not just as gatekeeper of the data, but also as someone who may have oversight of several areas of operation or several brands and frequently over many more years than the average brand manager. The sales force and R&D team are also usually very forthcoming with information typically at the simple cost of being asked and listened to.

In this process the planner can have a unique advantage by taking a much broader perspective on the issue. It may be as wide as drawing analogies with other market places (which is often surprisingly difficult from the client side yet should be very easy from the agency's experience base) or as simple as putting the brand into its wider context. If we are selling bolognese sauce, do we understand the full context of this and other pasta meals; where does it stand in the wider repertoire of Italian cooking; what meal occasions are we competing for and against what other foods; how does preparation time and the availability of ingredients affect decision-making; how does family context and preparer's mood contribute to meal choice?

The decision whether to support a brand is also made in a wider context which it would be too simplistic to ignore. What other brands are in the portfolio and how should priorities be allocated between them? Will supporting one brand benefit others in the portfolio or will it detract from their sales? What else is competing for the money internally? It may not just be shareholder value but the decision to install new plant or to modify the logistics system or to invest in the research and development of the next generation of brands. Clearly the planner can't expect to be an expert in all operational areas but it helps to avoid naïveté in the debate if the range of other spending possibilities is at least acknowledged and understood. Sign-off, particularly for media budgets, often involves millions of pounds and these decisions will only be taken at the highest level within a company. The ability to make the broader arguments (often on behalf of the marketing team who will be presenting them internally) goes a long way to protecting the long-term interest of the brand and, therefore, ultimately protecting both the client and agency source of revenue. Equally the planner must be informed and realistic about what advertising can and cannot achieve for a brand.

The role of brand champion extends beyond arguing the case for communication budgets. The planner must also be championing the right kind of support for the brand and the right content. This will be arrived at by an intimate participation in the business thinking process that surrounds any brand.

Contribution to business thinking

It has become a cliché to state that marketing is a discipline under pressure. For the first time in its relatively short life the value of a marketing department within a company has come under close scrutiny; there are several reasons for this. Few marketing departments are as big as they were in the 1980s and they are all under more stringent

Tesco	8.5m cards
Sainsbury	5.5 m cards
Safeway	4m cards

Figure 10.2: Supermarket loyalty cards

requirements to show effective and efficient use of budgets. Many now have fewer people to perform a more rigorous function. Almost every company has a financial representative on the main board, only a minority of companies have a marketing representative in that forum. The number of means of communicating with customers and potential customers has never been greater, there is fragmentation of existing media and proliferation of new media. Retailers have better access to data (through EPOS and loyalty schemes[2]) (see Figure 10.2) than ever before and usually a closer relationship with consumers. The growth of retailers as brands in their own right has meant that they have frequently moved from being 'customer' to being 'competitor' as well. All of these pressures on marketing mean that there is a premium on high quality thinking which leads to optimum communication with the target market (or, more frequently, more than one target market).

This pressure on marketing provides an opportunity for the planner to contribute to the broader 'planning' process and to become indispensable to the clients' business development. This goes beyond long-term brand thinking and cultivates a long-term client–agency relationship which can have a life outside the confines of individual brands.

The planner has the ability to bring in thinking from other markets or other territories. This is one of the key benefits of the breadth of agency experience whilst the client has to immerse himself in depth knowledge of his own particular industry. The understanding gained from service accounts helps fmcg companies by recognising that a brand these days needs to go beyond the product in order to fulfil or exceed customer expectations (e.g. when buying even everyday items such as margarine or soup, customers expect the brand to do more for them than simply supply an excellent product. So packs come with telephone numbers to contact care lines, to get further information, or indeed to get recipes or other similar inspiration). In the other direction, service companies can benefit from years of husbandry of brand values within fmcg accounts (particularly the imperative that brand delivery must live up to brand promise, a hard lesson for banks etc. to learn when the intermediary between brand and customer is a person rather than something rolling off the end of a well-managed production line).

Within the client–agency relationship who has the responsibility to think about the future? Part of the long-term stewardship of the brand is to ensure that it is fit to meet the demands of the next generation of users. It may be that the product or service which today is the manifestation of the brand will not be right for tomorrow. It is not true that brands must pass through a life cycle leading inevitably to decay and death. The changing pace of society and technology, however, do make it increasingly unlikely that the products and services which make up those brands can survive for ever in their current forms.

The day-to-day running of a brand rarely leaves the time for brand management to peer carefully into the future for possible opportunity or threat scenarios. There was a time when large insurance companies would state confidently that it would never be possible to sell insurance over the telephone: Direct Line quickly established market leadership with a telephone-only service, Virgin and Scottish Widows are now taking it even further with life insurance and pensions by phone. It was long believed that the British consumer would not be prepared to pay for television other than by the licence fee: BSkyB have not only established the habit of paying for programming by subscription but have pioneered pay per view television with the Bruno-Tyson boxing match. This external perspective can be effectively applied by the planner and brought to life with reference to other, possibly analogous, market places. The planner will also be using other outside sources to enliven interest in the outside world and the future. Books, reports, conferences, seminars all provide easy ways to pick up information or ideas which the client might not be exposed to without the planner's help. Sometimes a simple reference and other times an insightful piece of secondary analysis will win useful brownie points from a time-harried client.

The planner has the right to challenge conventional wisdoms and to ask 'What if?' questions. The creation of new products and services can often arise from turning the telescope round and viewing the problem from the other end; we probably spend far too much time altering the focus of our attention on increasingly small aspects of a problem – what if, instead of getting further into the minutiae we took a much broader view of the issue and challenged the prevailing 'givens' in the market place? So for example in a world of dieting and health concerns there is a big opportunity for indulgence ice creams (Haagen Dazs). When financial institutions are busy rushing into each other's markets there is a niche for an ethical bank (Co-operative Bank).

Competitive monitoring fulfils a similar role in preparing the client for dealing with his market place. Competitive monitoring should go beyond the collection of competitive advertising material and spend. What new products are being launched, what is being written about the market and what are competitors saying about their activities in public media, in annual reports and even on the grapevine? It is often proper from an internal perspective for competitors to be looked down upon and their capabilities denigrated. The planner has the right to be the devil's advocate and to see things from the competitive perspective. How would Marks and Spencer approach this issue, what would Virgin do if they were entering your market? Thinking and best practice about brand management, brand development and brand elasticity are constantly evolving; the planner has the greater responsibility within the agency team to feed and inform the client and to sponsor the debate on the need to change.

The planner should also be bringing in new ways of thinking and techniques for problem-solving. Because of the perceived objectivity of the planner there is often the opportunity to play the role of the third party. This can take the form of moderating brainstorm sessions or facilitating workshops. There is plenty of literature in this area and a plethora of techniques to 'borrow' for use within the client company. Creative problem-solving is something that planners do within agencies and they should extend these approaches and techniques into their clients. It is an expertise that is relatively easily learned and practised and yet often not to be found within client companies.

More companies are subscribing to the view that problems are best approached from a multidisciplinary team point of view. It is being increasingly recognised that marketing is the job of the whole company and not simply of a single department. Other disciplines such as sales, research and development, manufacturing and finance are being drawn into the process in a more formal way. The process of active analysis which occurs in workshops and awaydays is an ideal way of getting into the company beyond the marketing department. Active analysis means the live handling of problems with the problem owners in a round table session where the solution is undetermined and will result from the discussions taking place (this is in contrast to the old-fashioned agency awayday which was more likely to be a series of presentations designed to impose one point of view over another). If the planner brings together and moderates these sessions then they are important routes into the wider aspects of the client's business (which often allow contacts to be made which prove useful later when gathering information to put together a brief or an IPA effectiveness case). Where a multidisciplinary team has come together to solve a problem, ownership of the solution by the whole team is much more easily gained; everyone was in the room as the solution emerged – there is no sell in afterwards to a 'not invented here' audience.

Planning communication strategy

The phrase 'integrated marketing' has become axiomatic and universal and yet is not a new concept. Ed Nay's acquisition strategy at Young and Rubicam in the 1980s put together a group comprising PR (Burson Marsteller), corporate identity and design (Landor Associates), direct marketing (Wunderman), sales promotion (Cato Johnson), medical communications (Sudler and Hennessey) as well as the main advertising agency Y & R. This group was able to handle a client's every need for marketing communication with a strategy that was christened 'whole egg' thinking. Other marketing services groups have formed using analogies such as orchestras to indicate their ability to play an integrated tune. The ability to deliver an integrated message to the consumer depends less on the ability to fulfil 'downstream' communication requirements (which of course include the historically 'below the line' media of promotions, direct marketing etc. as well as new media such as web site, computer games etc.) than the ability to engage in upstream conversations about the overall communication strategy. Unless agencies are invited to dine at this table the whole egg will remain a delicacy that is available to clients but rarely tasted. The logic of designing an integrated communication package depends on the marketing strategy and communication objectives agreed with the client – not solely on the agency's ability to deliver through diverse media. It should also be borne in mind that the success of integration should be measured at the receiving end (i.e. the consumer) and not at the executional end. [A personal example illustrates the difference. I had driven a Land Rover Discovery for almost two years when I received a mailing from my garage: if I replaced my Discovery with them I would get 12 months free servicing. That felt very good, relevant timing, motivating offer, a reward for being a good customer. Imagine my disappointment on seeing the same offer in the national press the next day, I wasn't a 'valued' customer after all because the offer was open to everyone. I expect that the agency thought they had done a good job of integration because the private and the public messages were saying the same thing. However as the recipient it did not feel in the least integrated because the different media gave the same message a completely different feel for me as a customer.]

The planner can build an 'ends'-based model by working closely with the client to understand what needs to be achieved. Participation in the creation of the marketing plan would be an ideal situation for the planner allowing a better understanding of what is really important to the business. In the real world time and relationships rarely allow this; the planner should, however, seek the client's co-operation in access to the plan on the agency's behalf. From here the planner can help to define the role that communications can play in achieving the business plan. There is little premium in optimism, realism is of more value. If realistic objectives are set for communications then they are more likely to be achieved and budgets justified. It is better to debate the relevance of communication in the planning phase than to wait for the argument when the audit and tracking data are on the table.

Once the right objectives have been set the roles of the different communication possibilities need to be considered. Is it better to concentrate or divide the budget? Do we need to hit many people or fewer people more often? What sort of mood do we want people to be in when we communicate with them? At this point we shade off into areas discussed in earlier chapters. It is crucial that the planner understands the roles of the different communication levers and the interaction of them. There are few other points in the process where these decisions can be made. Notwithstanding the overlap with media planning and other communication disciplines, the planner who has been involved in the whole business process is best placed to be providing the client with balanced help in deciding between competing channels of communication. The client will be expecting a degree of objectivity in this debate and it is well worth considering the long-term interests of the agency in having an enduring relationship versus the short-term interest of channelling funds through a particular medium.

The tools for allocating budgets between the different communication channels are rudimentary and thin on the ground. A good deal of first principle thinking still needs to be done in each case (see Chapter 2). Again the account planner (working with media planners and other communications disciplines) is probably in the best position to lead this debate. This is something of enormous value to clients as it comes back to their imperatives to make marketing appropriations efficiently. It is almost always the case that decisions on choice of media and levels of relative spend will have more effect on the outcome of communications than the minute attention to copy detail which, although important, is apt to occupy many hours of heated debate.

Having driven down the various communication routes and considered budget allocation the planner is in a position to share the briefing process with the client. The advertising agency brief has long been the preserve of the account planner but in the new world of communications the planner has the opportunity to participate in the briefing of the other communication disciplines. This has obvious advantages if the other disciplines are within the agency or its group, but is clearly also immensely valuable if not. The need for consistency in brand communication has never been formally proven but few practitioners would argue against it. With fragmented media the need to oversee both strategic and creative direction has probably never been greater. Where the planner has the client's trust s/he can genuinely expect to be involved in the briefing and synergy control across all communication and packaging etc. (See Figure 10.3.)

Figure 10.3:
Marketing communication is a conversation between a brand and its audiences

Effectiveness and accountability

The first step to measurement of effectiveness should already have been taken by the setting of clear and realistic objectives. A previous chapter dealt with the whys and wherefores of campaign evaluation but it is a subject of ever-increasing importance within the client's business. A good client relationship will allow all the possible data pointing to effectiveness (or otherwise!) to be collected. As well as access to sales data and analysis there are also 'soft' factors which can be used as evidence; what are the sales force saying about the campaign; what is the trade feedback, how do the employees feel about it? All of these can be as useful within a company as decimal point changes in a tracking study. There is often more data available than is currently or easily referred to. One retailer could never extract sufficient data to 'prove' the value of advertising. Until one Christmas when one of the TV regions ran the wrong copy giving a wrong date for the start of the New Year sale. When the legal document claiming compensation was put together it had a very full and rigorous analysis of the amount of sales lost due to the advertising being wrong. Shame that they had never been able to do this when the advertising was 'right'!

The value of effectiveness data should be clear from the earlier discussion of marketing appropriation. If a client does not have the evidence that the communication programme is working it will be increasingly difficult to justify next year's budget. The case for investing in communications has to pull its weight alongside the cases for investment in other parts of the business.

The knowledge gained from understanding how communications have worked is also a crucial feedback for strengthening the client relationship. The learnings gained make the planner's contribution to the next round of the planning cycle that much more valuable and helps to secure the agency's position as an indispensable business partner.

Within the overall effectiveness calculation it may be necessary to attempt to disaggregate the impact of different parts of the communication mix. Econometrics and similar modelling techniques[3] come into and out of fashion. Once again the planner can provide advice to an uncertain client about the worth and relative merits of different modelling approaches. This kind of expertise still resides within more agencies than client companies as it may fall across several of the agency's accounts. Transferring knowledge learned elsewhere can be very impressive and helpful to a client who rarely has resource to complicated mathematical tools. The IPA's own Advertising Works series are a useful source of reference and practical case studies which can be used to give clients confidence in some of the modelling techniques used.

Research

The last thing that most planners want to be is a cheap substitute for the client's research department, and this is rarely good business for agencies. However the link between planning and research is obvious and it is an area where the planner can bring a great deal of added value to the relationship. This can and should extend beyond the area of communications research, any data can be relevant in understanding the full business picture and, then, in developing more effective communications. Planners are often in a position to meet a wider range of researchers and can introduce new skills or specialisms or new techniques into a client.

A fresh pair of eyes on a research report or research de-brief can often bring useful new interpretation; research done on a specific topic may well yield data that is relevant to a different problem or opportunity. Planners can also assist market research functions in maintaining overall quality control. There are some questions that market research is just not well suited to answer; persuading enthusiastic young brand managers of this often requires a lot of dedication.

The agency also has an obvious interest in being represented when research for evaluating or monitoring communications is being discussed. It is likely that agencies have wider and more frequent contact with relevant suppliers and techniques and therefore have a valid contribution to make to the internal client debate. The right to participate in this debate will have been won in relation to other advice given on research. Even the most naïve research manager will be suspicious of the planner who only concerns himself with communications research, the agency's interests are usually very self evident.

The days when agencies could afford to sponsor large-scale research projects themselves are over for all but the very largest multinationals. However, small projects or participation in syndicated studies are both ways of entering the market research debate. Contact with the client is vital whether there is a market research department or not. If there is a department then they can be good allies, if there is no department then more help can often be offered. However, this section began with a warning not to become a cheap substitute for a research department and the line must be drawn in a sensible place.

Summary

A checklist for inputs into the client's business:

- Focus the debate on ends as much as on means.
- Know the client's market better than the client.
- Stay close to the client and his planning process.

- Be involved in the decision about which communication tools to use.
- Proof of effectiveness buys the right to participate.

Having a valued input into your client's business will help you to create a better relationship with your client which is in the interest of your agency for the long term. This relationship and understanding will lead to more efficient distribution of the budget across the communications means available. A better understanding of the business and the market will lead to better and more effective creative work across any communication channel. Demonstration of this understanding will give the client more confidence in the creative work and help the agency to sell the right solutions more often. Time invested in the client's business will pay back in the long-term relationship that all agencies profess to seek in the current environment. The planner has an immense role in cementing the agency/client relationship and, therefore, in securing the business in the long term.

11 Planning in other communications industries

Michael Harvey

There's more to life than advertising!

Working in advertising is one of the more enjoyable ways of earning a living. It is challenging, creative, exciting and rewarding. It is also seen as *important* by the top people in many well-known blue chip companies. It was the Chairman of BA himself, Sir Colin Marshall, who forced the agency review that led to one of the most momentous advertising account moves of the 1990s.

It is very easy, therefore, when working in advertising, to see it as the key communication tool for clients and become somewhat blinkered to what else is happening in the 'other communications industries'. But times are changing and the very fact that this chapter did not exist in the original edition of *How to Plan Advertising* is recognition that fundamental changes have taken place in the world of communications in the last ten years that those who work in or have an interest in planning advertising need to be aware of.

So what are those industries and what has changed to merit the inclusion of a chapter on them?

The changing communications scene

The 'other communications industries' divide into three broad areas:

- direct marketing (including sales promotion);
- public relations (including sponsorship);
- design.

Two major changes have taken place in respect of these industries over the last ten years. First, they are now taking a larger slice of clients' communications budgets. Nobody can agree on exactly how much extra share of the total budget these industries now have compared with ten years ago, but nobody disputes that there has been a significant increase.

The second key change is a greater appreciation of the benefits to clients of 'synergy' between the various communication tools available. This is partly a collective outbreak of common sense in the marketing community but it has also been driven by declining real advertising budgets (particularly for fmcg goods) which has forced marketers to seek ways of 'extending the message' cost-efficiently to consumers.

Indeed there are those who see the changes over the last ten years as a precursor to a new era of 'total' or 'integrated' communications where advertising is only one part of a much larger process and where the advertising agency would lose its dominant position as 'lead strategic agency' for the brand. This scenario clearly has implications for advertising account planning and is worth examining in more detail.

From synergy to integration?

In the heady days of the mid-1980s (a time some now look back on as the 'golden era' for advertising) very few people in advertising would even think about the other elements of a brand's communication beyond its advertising. Very occasionally one would be asked to brief the client's direct marketing agency on a creative idea to enable them to create some synergy but little more than that.

The benefits of creative synergy in communications are now widely accepted. A creative idea will work harder if it is seen not just in advertising but also in other aspects of the marketing mix. I was always bemused when working on the Dulux account in the mid-1980s why the Dulux dog (which by *that* time had been an advertising icon for nearly 20 years) did not appear on packs. It does now.

But this 'advertising-led' synergy where the strategy and creative idea developed by the advertising agency is passed on to the direct marketing, PR and packaging design agencies is seen to have a fundamental flaw by a new breed of 'integrated' agencies. They believe that the advertising agency will favour above-the-line media in its planning. Their vision is of a common communications *strategy* for a brand being developed which would first be a template for deciding which media and communications tools should be employed and then act as the common brief for all the communication tools selected.

In this new era there would be no logic for a book to be called *How to Plan Advertising*; rather the title of this book would be *How to Plan Communications*.

The future of the 'integrated' agency

Although, in theory, there is much to commend the concept of 'integrated' agencies, in practice the dominant force in the organisation of communications in the next millennium is likely to remain the advertising agency.

The heart of this debate is *not* about the value of integrated communications, few in advertising would dispute its value; the debate is about who acts as the 'lead strategic agency' in the process and who does the creative work for the various communications tasks.

The 'integrated' agency offers total communications strategy development and all the creative (advertising, direct etc.) in one place. However, very few of the larger clients are comfortable with this. They do not believe that one agency can be the best creatively in all the communications disciplines. Clients' own organisational structures can also militate against this, with the large clients often having in-house specialist buyers for the different communications tasks.

The debate then becomes focused on the issue of 'lead strategic agency'. Although a new breed of 'brand strategy consultancy' is currently gaining credence with clients, the advertising agency is still best placed to act as 'lead strategic agency'. The planning function has long been integrated into their cost structures, allowing them to provide on-going strategic services to clients that others cannot.

Thus, while the desire for integrated strategic solutions will continue, clients will also by and large continue to seek 'best creative' from different suppliers. In these circumstances, there is no real reason why advertising agencies and, in particular, advertising agency planners should not continue to dominate the strategic development process as long as they take a broader view of communications and understand their potential role in respect of the other communications disciplines. In the rest of this chapter we examine the role of the other communications disciplines and how planning relates to them.

Direct marketing

The role of direct marketing

Direct marketing is defined by O&M Direct as 'activity which creates and exploits a direct relationship between our clients and their customers, or prospects, as individuals'. They stress that their primary accountability is to (sales) results and their motto is 'We sell – or else'.

In years gone by this aspect of communication tended to be known as 'direct mail' as this was the focus of its activity. Agencies would buy the use of what they thought were suitable lists of people to mail to and prepare a 'mailshot'. It was not very sophisticated either in terms of targeting or the sophistication of the mailing piece.

Today life is somewhat different. Not only do we have a smarter consumer who has been bombarded with 'junk mail' for years but we have much more effective direct marketing techniques. The explosion of computer power has allowed much greater individual targeting of consumers which not only increases the efficiency of direct marketing but is also in tune with one of the core consumer needs of the 1990s, the desire to be recognised as an individual.

Sales promotion is also an aspect of direct marketing. It used to be an entirely separate discipline concerned only with generating short-term sales uplifts and its effect was often nullified in the longer term by competitors' promotions. Sometimes, particularly in the case of durables, all it managed to achieve was to 'pull forward' sales that would have happened anyway. Nowadays sales promotion is often the start of a name capturing process that feeds into a much more sophisticated direct marketing approach.

Existence of account planning in direct marketing

A survey of the top 20 direct marketing agencies conducted in 1996 revealed six as having an account planning function in their own right. This is the highest incidence of account planning outside of advertising and confirms direct as one of the more sophisticated of the 'other communications industries'.

Caution needs to be exercised in assessing whether a direct marketing company has account planning as there is another function in direct marketing that is also known as 'planning'. This is the *database* planning role. The creation, or purchase, and the manipulation of consumer databases is at the core of direct marketing. The stratification and segmentation of databases, the targeting of subsets of these, the analysis of response to direct activity and the reclassification of consumers in the light of that response are all sophisticated data processing tasks and the person responsible for such activity in a direct marketing agency is often known as the planning director or manager.

Even where there is a genuine *account* planner, however, the role in a direct company is somewhat different to that of the advertising agency planner.

Role of account planning in direct marketing

Account planning's role in direct marketing is influenced by the relationship that direct companies have with their clients and the way that they are funded. This differs fundamentally from the way advertising agencies operate.

In advertising, clients enter into medium- to long-term relationships where the income flow (either fees or commission) has some degree of certainty. This allows a planning function to be funded as part of the overall service and as planning is expected as the 'norm' by clients, advertising agencies have long since adjusted their internal cost structures to accommodate it.

In direct, planning is not the norm. Contracts are invariably awarded on a one-off project fee basis and are also of lower value than a typical advertising project. In these circumstances account planning has to be constantly justified as it is charged as a cost against the project.

Thus, the first difference for the account planner in direct is that he or she is usually offering a project-based planning service and there tends to be a far higher ratio of accounts (or projects) per planner. Clearly it is also very difficult to build up the same ongoing depth of knowledge as the advertising planner as the moment the project is concluded, no more time can be charged against it. In advertising the 'team' continues to work between bursts of advertising and often when an execution runs unchanged for several bursts, the agency will justify its ongoing commission or fee by taking planning initiatives! There are no such luxuries for planners in direct.

Another major difference for planners in direct is in the status that they enjoy. In advertising the planner (with the account director) is effectively providing free marketing support for clients. It is an undeniable fact that the great shake-out of British industry in the 1980s compounded by the devastating effect of the recession in the early 1990s left most clients leaner and more profitable. However in the process, marketing departments were decimated with ever more junior brand management having to cope with many more brands. In these circumstances the advertising agency (including the planner) with its wealth of marketing expertise is offered a seat at the top table by the client.

Direct is largely perceived by clients as a specialism and not one that is expected to provide marketing consultancy. The direct company often finds itself interfacing with junior brand management or the client's specialist 'direct' manager. Additionally there tends to be no culture of developmental qualitative research in direct, for very good reasons. It is usually cheaper to test a piece of direct communication in the marketplace than to pre-research it qualitatively (or even quantitatively) and the results will be far more predictive of the real world.

Indeed, many traditional direct marketers say that creative work itself is not the most important place for a direct company to leverage value for its client. With direct marketing, getting the targeting right will often have a greater impact on sales than getting a 'better' creative product. In the case of sales promotion a similar observation can be made. There are more sales from getting the mechanics of the offer right than getting a 'better' offer.

Skills required by the planner in direct marketing

Among the skills that would serve the account planner well in direct are clearly quantitative skills. These enable an understanding and analysis of databases focusing as much, if not more, on what the consumer does (i.e. behaviour) rather than on what he thinks (i.e. attitudes).

In the direct agencies where account planning has established itself more strongly there is normally a management commitment to the delivery of the 'great selling idea' and a belief that the development of that idea will be enhanced by the consumer insights provided by the account planner.

Whilst account planning in this more enlightened type of direct agency is more akin to advertising account planning, there are still some key differences. The problem of a larger number of smaller projects does not go away, with the result that the planner is frequently required to write many more briefs than in an advertising agency (or simply accept that many will be done by account handlers). The planner also usually has only a fraction of the time provided to an advertising agency to find out about the consumer (and often very little original research). The briefing form is no easier to complete than in an advertising agency as these more enlightened direct agencies tend to have (not surprisingly) creative briefing formats that are very similar to ad agencies. (See Figure 11.1.)

Client: Creative WIP Date:
Job number: Internal:
Media:
Media budget: Client presentation date:
Production budget:
Hours:
Management supervisor:
Account director:
Creative director:
Planner:
Attached is information in the following areas: (You must supply information in at least five areas)

Page 1 box:

Client: Creative WIP Date:

Job number: Internal:

Media:

Media budget: Client presentation date:

Production budget:

Hours:

Management supervisor:

Account director:

Creative director:

Planner:

Attached is information in the following areas:
(You must supply information in at least five areas)

☐ Publication   ☐ Orchestrational guidelines
☐ Current advertising   ☐ Executional guidelines
☐ Previous work   ☐ Product anecdotes
☐ Competitive activity   ☐ Contact strategy
☐ Research   ☐ Sales materials

Page 1

Page 2 box:

1. What's the brand positioning for all communications?

2. What's the role of direct marketing for this client?

3. What are the client's objectives for this job?

4. Who are we talking to?
   (demographic, attitudinal, behavioural)

Page 2

Page 3 box:

5. What do they actually think about our product/brand?
   (consumer perceptions, not product)

6. What do we want the consumer to think?
   (rational and/or emotional, i.e. desired brand image)

7. What do we want them to do?
   (single action point is best)

8. What is the proposition?

Page 3

Page 4 box:

9. Why should they believe this?
   (provide support for the proposition only, not a list of product features)

10. How should we be speaking to them?

11. How will the work be critiqued?
    (i.e. at WIP stage – not merely results)

12. Creative restrictions/inclusions

Page 4

Figure 11.1: Direct marketing creative brief

The Heinz case history

Interestingly, the most well-known direct marketing case history of recent years, Heinz, was the product of a direct marketing agency, WWAV Rapp Collins, that is not particularly known for its account planning.

The fame of this case history, particularly in advertising circles, rests on the fact that not only did a leading above-the-line advertiser decide to spend a large amount below the line but that it chose to fund it by stopping above-the-line advertising for individual products. Advertising agencies saw not only their budgets reducing but also their role as 'lead strategic agency'.

Heinz cites a number of reasons for reviewing its communications strategy. First, far from being 57 varieties, Heinz found that it had 360 varieties on sale, a number that simply could not be supported by conventional brand advertising. Second, media inflation and fragmentation were making conventional above-the-line advertising less efficient. Third, and perhaps most importantly for Heinz, the increasing power of the big retail groups, all of whom not only have very credible own brands but now also have robust customer databases and loyalty card programmes, raised the question of who owns the consumer relationship. The final reason was the decreasing cost of database technology (it is 500 times cheaper to process an item of information than 20 years ago) as well as being quicker.

For all of these reasons Heinz decided to stop individual product advertising and use direct marketing to bring individual product messages direct to their best customers. The idea was to target the heavy using consumers in Heinz's core categories. These were mainly young families with four-plus people in the household. There were five million such households or 23 per cent of the UK population and they represented just under 50 per cent of Heinz profit.

The plan was to build a database of as many of these people as possible and then to communicate product messages to them four times a year. The direct mailing piece was called 'At Home'. When consumers opened it up they found a personalised letter and a 16-page magazine about food, recipes, new products, hints on how to feed the kids and a number of individually personalised money-off coupons against a range of different Heinz products. There was also a self-completion behavioural questionnaire about brands purchased in each of Heinz's categories and frequency.

This allowed the database to be refined and segmented with everyone on the database 'scored' in terms of loyalty and frequency. Potential incremental profit per household per year for Heinz was calculated so, for example, a frequent purchaser but mostly of competitive products would have most potential. Finally by relating the household's redemption of individual coupons to the database, the most responsive of those with most potential could be targeted.

As the database became more sophisticated greater segmentation and targeting could take place with 'Kidz at home' and 'Baby at home' magazines being targeted appropriately. Having built the database and thereafter only needing to keep it running, Heinz was able to free up funds to supplement spend on its umbrella advertising campaign to keep the emotional good will of Heinz topped up. A campaign of ten-second commercials was created reflecting ordinary people using Heinz products in a way that gives clues to their job or hobby or some aspect of their personality. This campaign reflected a regular *At Home Magazine* feature of ordinary people using Heinz products but is fundamentally different from previous adverting in that it is a Heinz brand campaign, not an individual product campaign (albeit that individual products are featured).

Campaign evaluation in direct marketing

Evaluation in direct marketing is easier than in advertising as the objective is invariably to directly influence sales. Sales results (or enquiries) are thus the usual method of evaluation. However, as with advertising, it is not sufficient that sales went up among those targeted. The question of what they would have bought in any event and whether the extra sales outweighed the marketing cost must be calculated. The At Home evaluation is an example of how to verify the success of a more sophisticated direct marketing campaign.

To assess success, Heinz used the AGB Superpanel which has 8,500 housewives on it. By matching the 4.6 million Heinz records with AGB it was discovered that 2,500 members of Superpanel were on the Heinz database. These were then compared with a matched sample who were not on the database. This analysis showed that significant share increases were achieved across most categories, some as high as five or six per cent, which is a considerable achievement in a mature category.

Public relations

The role of PR

The role of PR can be divided into three broad areas – corporate communication in crisis situations, on-going corporate communication and brand communication .

It is in the first of these, crisis management, that PR tends to have its highest profile. In a takeover situation the target will be the City, the media and ultimately the shareholders but in a situation where, owing to some production line fault or contamination, a brand or product needs to be withdrawn from the market, the general public via the media will be the target.

The second area, ongoing corporate communication and media relations, is the bread and butter of the PR industry. Here the product is the company itself (not its brands) and the target consumer will usually be opinion formers and the financial community.

The third area, PR's role in *brand communication*, is potentially the most exciting role for PR and the area where planning could have most influence.

This can be purely about a conventional brand but increasingly in the future it will be about the 'corporate' brand as companies can no longer afford to support individual brands.

Existence of account planning in PR

It is rare to find a formal account planning function in the PR industry. In fact in our survey of the top 20 PR companies conducted in 1996 only one claimed to have an account planning function.

The reasons for this lack of formal planning can be found in the role that PR plays in communications and in the development and structure of PR companies themselves.

The (potential) role of planning in PR

When a PR company is involved in a crisis situation, it will usually put together a 'crisis management team'. Apart from the client and the client's technical experts, the team may include the advertising agency account director. The advertising agency planner will not usually be part of this team but I would argue that this is short-sighted. The planner has a wealth of knowledge of consumer attitudes and how they respond to communications, particularly in this marketplace, and can give valuable advice on the tone and content of the company's response to the crisis.

In on-going corporate communications the PR company tends to believe that it knows its consumers' requirements well and, apart from accessing any corporate image studies that will have been conducted, will see little need for 'planning' in the sense that advertising agencies understand it. The role that the advertising agency planner might play in these circumstances will depend on the closeness of the association between the parent company and the advertised brands. Where there is a weak link (as between Procter & Gamble and its advertised brands) the activities of the PR company will impinge less, if at all, on the brand's consumers but where the company name and its brands are inextricably linked (as for example with Cadbury) the advertising agency planner should be ensuring that the PR company is fully aware of brand positionings and personality derived for the advertised brands to attempt to ensure some synergy in the tone of voice adopted. This is absolutely essential for 'monolithic' brands where the corporate name is always used with product descriptors to create 'sub-brands' as is the case with Virgin (Virgin Cola, Virgin Vodka, Virgin Radio etc.).

The area of PR activity where planning could have most influence is where PR is recognised as having a role to play in ongoing *brand communication*. However, although a potentially key role for PR, it is not as dominant as might be hoped. The reason for this is two-fold. First, client structures and budgeting tend to militate against the incorporation of on-going PR as an element of the *brand* marketing mix (it is still seen as a corporate tool). Second, the state of development and structure of the PR companies themselves tends not to encourage it.

It is not unreasonable to say that PR is probably the least mature of the communications industries in terms of the way that it is structured. Whereas advertising has four frontline functions (account handling, planning, creative and media), direct marketing at least three (account handling, creative and database management), design and sales promotion at least two (account handling and creative), PR (as with sponsorship) tends to have only one. In a PR company the account handlers not only manage the account, they are also the strategists and the creatives. There is very little formal training in the various marketing disciplines, with the result that most people in PR tend to have a general understanding of brand communication rather than being specialists in any particular part of it.

Sponsorship

Sponsorship tends to operate in a very similar way to PR and the two disciplines are closely linked. Account planning is not used in sponsorship but the advertising agency planner clearly has a role in ensuring that the brand's positioning and personality are fully understood by the sponsorship agency. This will ensure a good fit between any event or activity sponsored by the brand and the rest of the brand's communications.

A new breed of PR company?

Although there are very few at present, a new breed of PR companies is emerging that are focusing not only on using PR as an integrated brand communication tool but also in employing their own planners to analyse the brand in a very similar way to how the advertising planner works. There is clearly great opportunity for liaison between the advertising planners and the PR planners in these new companies where they find themselves working on the same brand. With ever-decreasing advertising budgets in real terms, it will always be in the advertising agency's interests (and of course the client's) for the various parts of the brand's communications activity to be working synergistically.

As with all the 'other communication industries' the ratio of planners to accounts is less than in an advertising agency and, hence, the PR planner tends to focus more on those accounts where planning skills are most useful. These tend to be the fmcg accounts where the PR planner would often be part of a 'total communications team' put together by the client encompassing advertising, design, direct marketing and PR.

In this role the PR planner would have an input to the overall brand positioning and then interpret how that could be best expressed through PR. Given the lack of a separate 'creative department' in the PR company structure the planner's contribution to the PR solution could be considerable.

Despite this development, looking towards the future it is difficult to see major changes in the relationship between traditional PR and advertising. It is also unlikely that account planning will gain a major foothold in the PR industry overall.

esign

The role of design

The design industry consists of several distinct parts:

- 'Brand design' which mainly involves packaging design but also includes literature and publications.
- Corporate identity design.
- Design of the environment which includes retail design.
- Physical product design.

Some design companies offer several of these disciplines but most tend to be seen as specialists in one or other of them.

All of these aspects of design communicate to the consumer and should theoretically be 'planned' to ensure that a brand positioning and personality is arrived at before design begins. In practice it is packaging and corporate identity that are the most 'marketing literate' and the ones that an account planner in an advertising agency is likely to come across. They are also the only areas where account planning has gained a small but significant foothold.

Packaging has been defined as 'a three-dimensional manifestation of a brand's positioning'; however, not all clients or packaging design companies yet see it in this light. Corporate identity similarly should be 'a visual evocation of a company's positioning' but again while many design companies sell it in this way, many clients still seek an aesthetic rather than strategic solution.

Existence of planning in design

A survey of the top 20 packaging and corporate identity design consultancies conducted in 1996 revealed four that claimed to have an account planning function. However as there are a significant number of ex-advertising account people working particularly in packaging design, the concept of 'account planning' is reasonably well known even if there are few planners employed as such. Freelance planners are sometimes employed and those design companies that are part of a larger communication group that includes advertising do sometimes pitch together with, and benefit from, the planning resource at the advertising agency.

The beginning of the application of account planning techniques to design can be traced back to the mid to late 1980s at the Michael Peters design company when there was an influx of ex-advertising agency staff who introduced planning.

The role of planning in design

Although practised in only a minority of design consultancies, the account planning process in developing packaging or corporate identity is remarkably similar to planning in advertising. The initial stages of strategy development will be identical – analysis of quantitative data to understand the market situation and use of mainly qualitative research and projective techniques to understand the relationship the consumer has with the brand (or corporate brand) and how that relates to the competition.

However, as well as arriving at an understanding of motivating brand values and a positioning, the design planner will also want to investigate design equities at this stage. These are aspects of the brand's visual identity that are recognised by the consumer as communicating core values and so should be retained in any future design. There are category equities which are generic to the category but essential to establish the brand in its competitive set and brand equities which are associated uniquely with the brand. Various techniques are used in qualitative research to elicit visual equities but asking respondents to draw what they remember of a pack (using appropriate colours) is one of the most useful.

The creative brief for a pack or corporate identity design is very similar to that used in advertising. This is to be expected if the belief exists that a brand's visual identity should communicate a core proposition in the same way as advertising can. However, for food products an extra dimension should be on the packaging brief. In addition to the rational values and emotional values, food packaging needs to communicate sensory values – the mouth-watering enjoyment of actually consuming the product.

The packs for the highly successful relaunch of Birds Eye's chicken range are an example of the evocation of sensory values in packaging. The packs capture visually (through colour and graphic devices) one of the most appealing sensations of eating chicken – the moment when the chicken leaves the oven and the aroma of freshly cooked chicken evokes the anticipation of an exceptionally enjoyable eating experience. (See Visual 11.1.)

Similarly, Tango packaging captures the individual taste sensations of each of its flavour variants – the 'hit' of the oranges, the 'seduction' of the apples experience, the 'euphoria' of the lemons experience and the energy 'charge' of the blackcurrant experience. (See Visual 11.2.)

In briefing the designers the planner needs to add as much colour and texture to the briefing as possible. 'Mood boards' to represent the positioning are far more helpful than words on a brief. This is because the pack or corporate identity designer cannot fall back on words to execute the brief. His or her communication tools are visual – images, colours and shapes, implicit not explicit, abstract not rational.

Design companies tend to be relatively small compared with advertising agencies and if there is an account planner, he or she will often be the only one in the company, with obvious implications for the workload and the depth with which any individual project can be 'planned'. As with direct, the planner in design just does not have the capacity to work on every single brief that goes through the agency.

Packaging design

Design is a project fee-based business and very price-competitive. Clients still tend to divide the design industry, particularly on the packaging front, into those seen as more 'strategic' who will want to investigate positioning issues and either employ a planner or use the planning process, and those that are seen as more 'creative' who tend to pass the client's own brief directly to the designers and promise an outstandingly creative design solution. To planners in the 'strategic' agencies, this is somewhat frustrating as they see their design solutions as no less 'creative'.

Visual 11.1:
Birds Eye
Chicken pack

Visual 11.2:
Tango packs

In an ideal world packaging should be seen as another tool to position the brand in the eyes of the consumer. It should be working synergistically with the advertising and direct marketing to reinforce the agreed brand positioning and personality. However, in practice, packaging development is frequently left in the hands of the most junior brand manager who has been given a very limited budget. This leads to one of the biggest frustrations for the account planner working in packaging design. Many clients simply do not see the potential of using the pack as a communication tool in the same way as advertising. Their only criterion for the success of a pack is *impact* at point of sale.

This focus on 'stand out' is the philosophy adopted for many years by large US companies such as Procter & Gamble and Mars. It leads to packs that are recognised by the consumer but that add nothing to the communication of brand values. Nowadays in a world of little or no rational product differentiation, where brand differences are largely emotional and where advertising budgets to clearly establish those emotional differences are limited, it seems obvious that as much relevant emotional appeal should be put into the packs as possible.

Indeed in a world where most packaged goods brands can no longer afford to be supported above the line, the pack is frequently the *only* medium for communication with the consumer. In these circumstances, it certainly has to say more than just its brand name.

Corporate identity design

Corporate identity design is arguably the most fulfilling part of the design industry for the planner to be involved in. Here the client liaison point is usually the Chief Executive or Corporate Affairs Director and there is no difficulty in convincing the client that a thorough planning process to develop the strategy is required. The design company is the 'lead strategic agency' and once a brief is agreed the design company will usually be given adequate time (and resources) to do the job properly.

Increasingly, the corporate identity consultancy finds itself analysing the entire performance of the company, from how it treats its customers to how ecologically sound are the sources of its materials. This is in response to society's increasing expectations from companies as corporate citizens. The behaviour of public companies and institutions is under the media microscope as never before. An institution that changes its corporate identity without a genuine change in culture, values or performance will be rightly criticised for superficiality and for having the arrogance to believe that the public can be fooled by a design change into believing there is real change.

The Clean Motor Show – case history

As in advertising, some of the most creative work in design can be achieved for charity accounts where the client tends to be more open to a single-minded strategic solution executed in a highly creative way.

In the spring of 1999 the Ark Foundation, an environmental charity, will be staging the first international 'Clean Motor Show'.

Ark pioneered 'cleaner' detergents and is now embarking on an ambitious project to clean up the world's motor cars. The 'Clean Motor Show' will be a showcase for the world's motor manufacturers to demonstrate what steps they are taking towards the Ark vision.

The design consultancy was briefed to develop an identity for the show and the key consumer insight discovered by planning was that people will be prepared to buy 'clean' cars as long as they *perform* as well as existing cars

The brief was therefore 'vroom without the gloom' (of knowing you're polluting the world). The personality should be dynamic, exciting and fun; not 'worthy and dull' as so many green projects are.

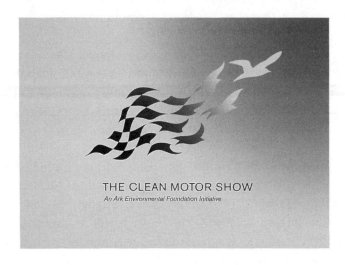

THE CLEAN MOTOR SHOW
An Ark Environmental Foundation Initiative

Visual 11.3:
Clean Motor Show

The creative solution was a chequered flag, the universal symbol of motoring performance, transforming into birds flying into a clear blue sky, thus at the same time implying both performance and cleaner air.

Researching design

Designers tend to come up with several rough concepts for the client presentation and then hone this down to two or three for qualitative creative development research. This research clearly needs sensitive handling as the communication of purely visual stimulus is difficult to assess. As with advertising there is a need to go well beyond what is 'liked', to discover what and how concepts communicate, if the research is to be meaningful and give insights to develop the design to finished form.

Evaluation of the exact *effectiveness* of design is often far more difficult than advertising as it is usually only one relatively small part of a complex marketing mix. For this reason the Design Business Association launched the Design Effectiveness Awards which are intended to convince marketers of the effectiveness of design in the same way as the IPA's Adverting Effectiveness Awards have for advertising.

A relatively sophisticated example of research to measure design effectiveness was that done for the Birds Eye Chicken relaunch. The relaunch at the beginning of 1995 had been a spectacular success with sales for the 12 months following the relaunch being 39 per cent higher than in the 12 months prior to relaunch.

Whilst pre-launch packaging research suggested that a significant part of the increased sales for Birds Eye must have been due to design, the exact amount was unknown as Birds Eye Chicken, like many leading food brands, advertises heavily. It was also in a market that is growing and again the question arose as to how much was 'natural' growth and how much caused by marketing activity. It was thus very difficult to build a case for design effectiveness using traditional methods.

To overcome the problem of numerous influences on sales, econometric modelling was used. The results of the modelling are shown in the chart below. From the beginning of 1995, after the new packs were in store, the model shows that sales are consistently 6 per cent higher than they would have been without the new packs.

Interestingly, the model also shows that sales were *adversely* affected by packaging during the four-month changeover period, which is not surprising as consumers would have initially been confused by the old and radically different new packs appearing side by side.

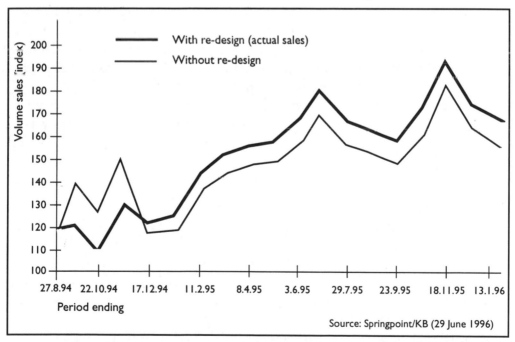

Figure 11.3: Birds Eye white meat sales: effect of packaging re-design

The model also analysed what made up the rest of the change in sales. It shows that the underlying trend towards healthy eating and white meat accounted for 11 per cent of the 39 per cent, or looked at another way, this was natural growth that would have come in any event. A further 10 per cent was due to new product launches (four new lines were introduced to the range in 1995) and Birds Eye's own advertising (and a reduction in competitors' advertising) added a further 11 per cent to sales.

Finally, the model showed that the design paid for itself out of incremental profits within the first few months of launch.

Summary and conclusions

All brand communication with the consumer contributes to (or detracts from) building the brand. Today more and more brand communication is happening outside of mainstream advertising. The logic of all communication – be it advertising, corporate identity, direct marketing, promotions, public relations, sponsorship or packaging design – all communicating the same positioning and personality for the brand, is inescapable.

The need to be more focused on positioning has led to an increase in the incidence of account planning in the 'other communications' disciplines over recent years but owing to both the organisational and financial constraints of these sectors it is still (and looks to remain) a minority activity.

The theoretically sound model of an 'integrated' agency that offers communications management, integrated strategic development and synergistic creative execution in all areas is only practised by a small minority. The majority of clients see the drawbacks of this system outweighing the advantages. However, brand strategy consultancies (who do not offer creative execution) are growing in clients' esteem.

While the more sophisticated agencies in the other communications disciplines are as capable as any advertising agency of developing a positioning and personality for a brand, the role of integrating strategy and communication is currently largely a client responsibility (and usually executed by a 'task force' of the different disciplines).

If advertising agencies wish to retain their status in clients' eyes as 'guardian of the brand' they should take a broader view of clients' needs for integrated communication solutions. For organisational, financial and historic reasons the advertising agency is well placed to co-ordinate this process for clients. A key player in any such 'communications co-ordination' would be the planner.

Notes and references

Chapter 1

Brown, G. (May 1991) 'Big Stable Brands, and Ad Effects'. *Admap.*
Brown, G. (January 1994) 'The Awareness Problem'. *Admap.*
Brown, G. (1991) 'Lessons from Advertising Tracking Studies'. MRS Seminar.
Brown, G. (1987) 'Campaign Tracking: New Learning on Copy Evaluation and Wearout'. ARF
    Workshop.
Brown, G. (April 1987) 'The Link Between Sales and Advertising Content'. *Admap.*
Channon, C. (March 1981) 'Agency Thinking and Agencies as Brands'.
Gibson, L. (March 1983) 'Not Recall'. *Journal of Advertising Research.*
Gordon, W. & Ryan, C. (1982) 'How Do Consumers Feel Advertising Works?' MRS Conference
    Papers.
Hedges, A. (November 1974, reprinted September 1982) 'Testing to Destruction'. *IPA.*
Lannon, J. (October 1985) 'Advertising Research: New Ways of Seeing'. *Admap.*
Meadows, R. (July/August 1983) 'They Consume Advertising Too'. *Admap.*
O' Brien, Dr T. (December 1984) 'What Consumers Bring to Advertising'. *Focus Research.*
Pollitt, S. (20 April 1979) 'How I Started Planning in Agencies'. *Campaign.*
Jones, J. P. (1996) 'Getting It Right First Time'. *Admap.*
Rainey, M. T. (1995) 'No Free Thinking'. *Adweek Solutions '95 Conference Papers.*
Rainey, M. T. (1994) 'The Agency Role In Marketing's Metamorphosis'. *ICM Conference Papers.*
Rainey, M. T. (1997) High Noon for the High Ground'. APG Conference Papers.
Smith, A. & Carter, M. (10 March 1997) 'Turf War: Agencies vs. Consultants'. *Financial Times.*

Chapter 2

Duckworth, G. (ed.) *et al,* 'Advertising Works 1–9', (NTC *et al,* 1981–1997).
King, S. 'Improving Advertising Decisions', (*Admap,* April 1977).
Ries, A. and Trout, J. *Positioning: The Battle For Your Mind,* (McGraw-Hill, 1981 and 1986).
Cowley, D. (ed.), *Understanding Brands,* (Kogan Page, 1991 and 1996).
Webb Young, J. *How To Become An Advertising Man,* (re-published 1963).

Chapter 4

Ghiselin, B. (1985) *The Creative Process,* US, California University Press.
Popper, K. R. (1992) *Unended Quest,* London, Routledge.
APG (1995, 1997) *Creative Planning: Outstanding Advertising.* Account Planning Group.

Chapter 5

'The Anatomy of Account Planning', *Admap,* November, 1989.

Chapter 7

Barwise and Ehrenberg(1985), 'Consumer Beliefs and Brand Usage', *JMRS* 27, 2 April.

Jones, J. P. (1995), *When Ads Work*, Lexington Books, Massachusetts.

O'Malley, D. (1991), 'Sales without salience? Small brands, advertising models – and the curse of television' , *Admap*, September.

Reeves, R. (1961), *Reality in Advertising*, Alfred A. Knopf, New York.

Further reading

There is a huge literature relating to the topic of advertising evaluation. I have kept this list as short as possible; anyone who wants to go further will find plenty of references in the first three titles mentioned.

John Philip Jones, *What's in a Name? Advertising and the Concept of Brands* (Lexington Books, Massachusetts, 1986) – scholarly but very readable. Although John is now a tenured Professor at Syracuse University, NY, he is British by birth and worked for many years at J. Walter Thompson in London.

Simon Broadbent, *The Advertising Budget* (NTC Publications in association with the Advertising Association, Henley-on-Thames, 1989), and *Accountable Advertising* (*Admap* Publications in association with the ISBA and the IPA, Henley-on-Thames, 1997) – practical guides on relating advertising to business results

Colin McDonald, *How Advertising Works* (NTC Publications in association with the IPA, Henley-on-Thames, 1992) – the best short overview of this perplexing subject, an understanding of which is closely bound up with questions of evaluation

There are two useful booklets published by the IPA (44 Belgrave Square, London W1): *Best Practice in Campaign Evaluation*, (1995), and *Advertising and Modelling – An Introductory Guide* (1989).

The nine volumes of *Advertising Works* ,including the introductions (since volume 6, published by NTC Publications with the IPA).

Whatever criticisms have been levelled at them, the IPA Advertising Effectiveness Awards have done a vast amount to raise the profile of the whole issue of advertising evaluation in this country. They also provide an unparalleled source of detailed case histories, and demonstrate a far wider range of possibilities than I have been able to cover in this chapter. Despite their daunting weight and small print, every planner should read them!

The most useful (and readable) journal is *Admap* from NTC Publications, where the issues raised in this chapter have been regularly debated for the past 30 years. It is probably the most effective way of keeping up to date with new developments in the field.

Chapter 8

1. *BRAD* is a monthly publication by the EMAP group which lists publications radio stations, television channels and outdoor media together with their advertising rates and information on their circulation, viewing, listening and so on. It costs £130 monthly and is an extremely useful reference for basic facts on the media. *BRAD*, Emap Business Communications, Chalk Lane, Cockfosters Road, Barnet, Herts, EN4 0BU.

2. **Media terms**

   IMPACT: In media terminology an IMPACT is defined as one person experiencing one exposure to an advertisement. However whilst this is an easy concept it is difficult to be precise about. For a magazine the National Readership Survey measures the readership of the average issue of a magazine, not whether a particular advertisement in a particular issue was seen. For TV the measure is 'someone in the room with a TV set switched to the said channel when the advertisement appeared – the data being captured electronically.

OTS: More commonly used is OTS or opportunities to see. This is the number of people who have had the opportunity to see the advertisement. If a TV campaign achieved 80 per cent coverage at five OTS this means that 80 per cent of the target audience would have had the opportunity to see the campaign at least five times.

TVR: Normally on television the OTS are expressed as a percentage of the total population and called Television Ratings. For women who have children the total number in the UK population is 6.76 million so our spot would achieve a TVR of 15, i.e. 15 per cent = 1 million as a percentage of 6.76 million. TVRs are additive and are used to measure buying performance i.e. how much was spent per TVR. So for example we could have bought eight spots as above and achieved a total TVR of 8 x 15 = 120 TVRs in total. It is important to remember that TVRs can be made up in many different ways and 120 TVRs could be 8 x 15 TVRs or 10 x 12 TVRs or any other combination of spots. In addition, although 100 TVRs is theoretically 100 per cent seeing once, it is always made up of smaller audiences seeing several times.

Coverage and frequency: Over a campaign some people will have the opportunity to see the advertisement more than others. The total number of people who saw the advertisement at all is called coverage and if we divided the total of all the OTS by the coverage we have the average frequency of the campaign. For more details on these and other terms see the Media Research Group *Guide to Media Research* edited by Colin McDonald and Mike Monkman, published by the Media Research Group 1995.

Target Group Index: A survey of the purchasing and usage habits of 24,000 people. It also includes data on their demographics and media use. It is carried out annually by personal interview and is published by BMRB Ltd. Consumer purchasing of brands can be compared in a large amount of detail with their media use.

BARB (Broadcasters Audience Research Board Ltd: BARB is shorthand for the data produced by electronic meters attached to the back of television sets of a panel of 4,435 homes. The meters measure the hours people view television and which channels they view, both commercial and the BBC. It is very detailed and provides data by the minute. The data is captured electronically from respondents who register their presence in the room via an attachment to their television sets. It covers all channels and also video viewing. The data is available overnight via computer links to the AGB computer who feed it out to computer bureaus who can be accessed by media companies. Thus results of TV buying are available overnight. BARB also manages an audience appreciation panel of 3,000 adults which is confidential to the BBC and commercial television companies.

Share of Voice (SOV): The per cent share of the total spend of that category that any advertiser achieved in the period studied. It can be expressed as a percentage of the money spent or a percentage of the total TVRs achieved by all advertisers in that sector.

Radio Advertising Bureau: There are approximately 140 commercial radio stations in the UK, and RAB (the marketing arm of the radio industry) provides an independent information service to advertisers. RAB, 77 Shaftesbury Avenue, London, W1V 7AD, Tel: 0171-306 2500, Fax: 0171-306 2505, http://www.rab.co.uk. They also produce an excellent book entitled *The Radio Advertising Handbook*.

Further reading

Jones, J. P. (1994), *When Ads Work*. New York: Lexington Books.McDonald, C. (July/August 1996) 'How Frequently Should You Advertise' *Admap*, pp. 22–25.Oxfordshire: NTC Publications Ltd.

'Hit The Target' – *Media and Marketing Europe – European Planning Guide, 1996*, pp. 12–15. London: Emap Business Communications.

Chapter 9

Levitt, T. (May–June 1983) 'The Globalisation of Markets'. *Harvard Business Review.*

With special thanks to:

Linda Caller, Ogilvy & Mather; Nick Kendall, Bartle Bogle Hegarty; Merry Baskin, J. Walter Thompson; Bob Roscow, Saatchi & Saatchi; Sue Moss, Saatchi & Saatchi; The Research Business; British Airways; Hewlett Packard; Zenith.

Chapter 10

1. There are a wide range of data sources available to clients. In fmcg companies they will typically have access to sales data by volume and value, expressed as absolutes and as market share. They will probably also know penetration, regionality, seasonality, distribution and rate of sale. These data as well as pricing information will be available for client and competitive brands. The main suppliers for this kind of information are still Nielsen and AGB Taylor Nelson. It is also likely that the client will have consumer-focused knowledge such as awareness, attitudes and behaviour from usage and attitude surveys and also softer understanding of consumer motivations and feelings from qualitative research studies. Another common source of data is the advertising tracking study which uses regular surveys of the target market in an attempt to identify the effectiveness of advertising communications.

    Non-fmcg manufacturers and service providers may have less rich data in the area of sales volume and share etc., but are otherwise likely to have similar sources. Service providers often use mystery shopping techniques to get an impartial measure of their quality of delivery. All advertisers will have some degree of desk research and published reports on their market place. There will also be some degree of internal data (ex-factory shipments, accounts opened, average sales value etc.) which may be useful for analysis.

2. All the major grocery multiples and an increasingly high proportion of all retailers now use some form of scanning products at the till. This provides a complete record of sales and is commonly referred to as EPOS data [Electronic Point Of Sale]. It gives the retailer an accurate picture of the quantity of sales and the rate of sales by the smallest detail; brand by flavour by size. It does this in real time and, therefore, knows when goods are selling and through which outlets. This information is very powerful in establishing which brands are selling well and provides the basis for Efficient Consumer Response [ECR] techniques such as 'just in time' deliveries which help to minimise inventory, out of stocks and therefore maximise profitability.

    Loyalty schemes have existed for many years (Air miles, petrol coupons, Green Shield stamps, Barclaycard Profiles) and are a technique used to persuade consumers to return to the same brand in return for rewards which accumulate the more you buy. They have returned to the mass market in a big way via the grocery multiples: Tesco with 8.5 million members of its Clubcard is the biggest, but Safeway and Sainsbury have now launched their own schemes. The schemes are a means of rewarding customers for regular shopping with cash refunds for points accumulated against spend. They are also a means of collecting an invaluable database of consumer information. When combined with EPOS data, the multiples now know exactly what each of its scheme customers is buying (and when, and how often, and how much etc.). This gives a complete record of sales by known individuals over time and is useful not only in maximising sales per individual but also provides a data-rich bargaining tool when dealing with suppliers.

3. Econometric modelling is a set of multivariate mathematical techniques often used to quantify the impact of advertising on sales. This technique is designed to disentangle all the factors that have historically influenced the level of sales; then the relative importance of each factor, including advertising, is revealed. Typically the advertising effect detected is small and rarely sufficient to be profitable in the short term. In the longer term advertising builds brand equity which is not so easy to measure. But econometrics can help here too. For example, it can analyse how changes in a brand's price sensitivity over time relate to levels of advertising.

Another way to measure the effects of advertising on sales is single-source data analysis. This is where the purchase behaviour of a panel of individuals is monitored over a long period of time and looked at in relation to their exposure to advertising. A substantial financial investment is required to build a single-source database but the technique can enrich understanding of actual consumer behaviour.

I should like to acknowledge the generous help in compiling this chapter of Stephen King, one of the Godfathers of planning from J. Walter Thompson. The mistakes, as they say, are of course mine.

Index